GROWING UP IN BOTSWANA IN THE 1930S & 40S

Tales of Adventure in Colonial Africa

BY SPENCER 'TED' NETTELTON

National Library of Australia Cataloguing-in-Publication entry
Author: Spencer 'Ted' Nettelton
Title: Growing up in Botswana in the 1930s & 40s
Subtitle: Tales of Adventure in Colonial Africa. Volume 1
ISBN: 978-0-9871911-8-2

© 2018 Spencer Enraght Nettelton. The content and all images in this book are subject to the copyright of their owner, Spencer Enraght Nettelton. No part may be reproduced by any process without written permission from the owner. Inquiries should be addressed to beverley.writer@gmail.com

These memoirs are dedicated to Gail, my late wife of thirty-five years, and to my three ever-attentive and loving daughters, Beverley, Tanika and Penny.

ACKNOWLEDGEMENTS

These memoirs owe much to the contributions and assistance from many people, but in particular I must thank Sarah Johnson, who did all my typing and layout over a period of at least ten years. Her patience was unlimited as I dawdled along. My daughters Beverley and Penny helped me enormously and Tanika, my other daughter, did her bit. Margaret's help with proofreading and grammatical structure is much appreciated, as is Pip Butler's lovely layout. Louise Moylan did my editing and layout for Books III and IV – such an efficient and easy to work with person.

I acknowledge the written contributions of Tony Turner, my brother-in-law, and my father's diaries and Uncle Geoff's memoirs were of course written by them.

Preface

At the outset a prime objective of my story was to describe how we lived on a day-to-day basis in those days and to paint a picture of the life of a British Colonial Officer serving in a British-governed African territory at the time of my service. It was a unique lifestyle which has now gone and will never return. To record this period through the eyes of a serving officer is a rare opportunity to make a contribution to social history. I intended to achieve the objective by detailing my own life in Botswana and Lesotho and that was it. But as I researched I realised there was a lot more than just my own life to be recorded; indeed there was a wealth of information about our forebears which was crying out to be brought together into a more cohesive family story, drawn not only from recent times but dating back in some cases hundreds of years.

I am grateful to those forebears who during their lifetimes wrote about themselves and their families. I trust those who come after me will value my writings just as I value the writings of my own forebears.

Dad's 1916-1924 Diaries are a fascinating account of his work as a Police Officer in what was then a remote Botswana with no electricity, telephones, motor cars or radio but teeming with wildlife. He lived a hard life with few creature comforts but he very seldom complains. This diary is now one hundred years old and I see it as a priceless and honest record of his life in those days.

Uncle Geoff, Dad's elder brother, wrote a 220-page account of his life – early days up to age fourteen growing up in remote Botswana. He subsequently fought in three theatres of war – the First World War, the Second World War North African campaign (leading to three and a half years in a prisoner of war camp in Germany). He finished the war as a Lieutenant-Colonel in charge of the Kaffrarian Rifles. Uncle Geoff obviously handled people well and got out of the front lines of the battle. He was not one to be sitting in his office directing the operations of his men from afar.

As seen from his own perspective, his account of the battle of El Alamein and the Siege of Tobruk, both of which he fought in, are fascinating.

Introduction

Spencer Enraght Nettelton

Known as Ted
Born February 7, 1932

I am now into my eighties and the time has come for me to bring together and finalise all the family data I have collected. Time is running out!

Some years back I sat down and dictated a two-hundred page blow-by-blow account of my life. As I wrote and researched I realised that I was just one person among a host of interesting and adventurous forbears. On all sides of the family we served in the British Army, Indian Civil Service and British Colonial Service, and in other capacities too, which took us to remote corners of the British Empire — often dangerous and arduous — and sometimes fatal.

Some of our relations have carried out research and gathered a lot of interesting data. I found family trees for various branches of the family, which sometimes date back to William the Conqueror (1066) and even before, but there seems to be nothing co-ordinated, with loose bits of paper and fascinating photo albums (the latter covering more recent times) lying around. With an ever greater likelihood that much of it would be relegated to a bottom drawer in someone's study and never looked at again, I was concerned not to see broken that thread of knowledge with the past which can interpret and explain and put the stories together as oldies like myself passed on. How I would like to sit down and chat to Dad and my aunts and uncles — we always seem to leave it too late.

My own detailed memoirs and those of Uncle Geoff, as well as Dad's diaries, are voluminous and need time to be read in full. Fascinating as they are, I felt it was necessary in certain instances to present them in an easily readable form and to link photos wherever possible. To reiterate what I have said in my Preface, at the forefront of my mind was to record the way we

British Colonial Officers and our families operated on a day-to-day basis both on official duties and recreation, ie at work and play.

With this in mind, in some instances I sought simply to tell a story about interesting events. I have tried to make this chronicle an easy read that can be delved into and put down, and hopefully a few more sections to read on other occasions.

We were British and by the middle of the 19th century half of the population of the world either belonged to the British Commonwealth of Nations (South Africa, Canada, Australia, New Zealand) or was governed from Whitehall. Most of our more immediate forbears found their way to southern Africa or India and their adventures and stories have this common background. I find it all immensely interesting – we were an adventurous lot! I hope you find it interesting too.

In writing my memoirs there is encouragement from the poem "If" by Rudyard Kipling. Why do I bring him into my memoirs? I have always enjoyed the writings of Kipling which so epitomised the spirit of colonialist Britain when at the zenith of its power. I unashamedly admit that I am proud to have been a member of the British administrative structure which governed so many of the British colonies spread around the world, and in our family heritage there are many others who , like me, were very much involved in British colonial issues whether in the military, government administration or private commercial enterprise.

Kipling's verse "If" portrays to me the image of an adventurous, brave and honourable man of that era and I would have been proud to have been likened to such a man. It would be fashionable in our modern era to demonise him as a "white colonialist oppressor". I was there and I never felt like an oppressor. I left the British Colonial Service with no feelings of guilt, rather with pride, because in Lesotho we left behind a system of administration which functioned.

If – Rudyard Kipling

If you can keep your head when all about you
Are losing theirs and blaming it on you,
If you can trust yourself when all men doubt you,
But make allowance for their doubting too;
If you can wait and not be tired by waiting,
Or being lied about, don't deal in lies,
Or being hated, don't give way to hating,
And yet don't look too good, nor talk too wise:

If you can dream—and not make dreams your master;
If you can think—and not make thoughts your aim;
If you can meet with Triumph and Disaster
And treat those two impostors just the same;
If you can bear to hear the truth you've spoken
Twisted by knaves to make a trap for fools,
Or watch the things you gave your life to, broken,
And stoop and build 'em up with worn-out tools:

If you can make one heap of all your winnings
And risk it on one turn of pitch-and-toss,
And lose, and start again at your beginnings
And never breathe a word about your loss;
If you can force your heart and nerve and sinew
To serve your turn long after they are gone,
And so hold on when there is nothing in you
Except the Will which says to them: 'Hold on!'

If you can talk with crowds and keep your virtue,
Or walk with Kings—nor lose the common touch,
If neither foes nor loving friends can hurt you,
If all men count with you, but none too much,
If you can fill the unforgiving minute
With sixty seconds' worth of distance run,
Yours is the Earth and everything that's in it,
And—which is more—you'll be a Man, my son!

I believe judgment of our British rule should be made on the basis of whether or not the ordinary person in the street is better off now than they were in colonial days, not solely on the basis of the political freedom of the elite few to make decisions for the running of the country and control of its economy which all too often entails maximising their own wealth and privilege with little regard for the ordinary citizen. This is not the case in all countries but any fair-minded person would have to concede that it is nevertheless a widespread problem.

The hostility towards the British Empire is particularly orchestrated by a group of journalists, historians and film makers who accentuate those issues which were not to the credit of the Empire (and in every history of every nation there will be good and bad) but say little or nothing about the good that was achieved.

I strongly contend that much of what has been written is not fairly balanced. And I further contend that the views of the ordinary citizen of a newly independent state should not be sought in the early days of nationalistic fervour but a decade or so down the track when the reality of "freedom from the British yoke" can be more accurately gauged against the quality of life under the new regime of independence. And those views should be ascertained not just from the upper echelons of the community but also from the ordinary person in the street.

In writing my memoirs there is encouragement from the Lord:

Put this on record for
The next generation,
So that a race still
To be born can
Praise God, know what has gone before.
Psalm 102 : 18 (J.B.)

Memoirs of Spencer Enraght Nettelton

At age four.

I was born on the 7th February 1932 in Francistown, Botswana, where my father Gerald was at that time a District Commissioner in the British Colonial Service. A midwife came up from South Africa to assist my mother for two or three weeks after my birth, which took place in the Residency. I weighed 9 lbs 3oz — my poor mother! There was, in fact, a resident medical officer in Francistown and presumably he also officiated. For years I had my own children and wife believe there was a brass plaque on the door of the Residency in Francistown to commemorate such a memorable event, but ultimately, much to their disappointment, I had to disillusion them that I was only pulling their leg.

I was the third child in the family. My brother Gerald was eighteen months old and my sister Elizabeth just on three years. It is worth commenting that in Sir Charles Rey's book *Lord of All I Survey*, he makes reference to a visit to Francistown where he stayed with my parents and he comments that Elizabeth and Gerald were the worst-behaved children he had ever come across! I think this is a bit unfair because we were in fact a well-disciplined and well-adjusted family, and I just think Sir Charles was having a bad day or Elizabeth and Gerald just didn't happen to be on their best behaviour.

Not long after my birth the family moved to Serowe, Dad once again District Commissioner and Magistrate. Dad was a fluent linguist in Sechuana and did not require an interpreter in court. His fluency was such that he could speak in the local idiom and was therefore never at a loss to fully understand what was being said. He was known by the indigenous people of Botswana as *Ngwato*, which means a person of the country. I guess this was a pretty complimentary reference to make towards him. In references to him in the many books that have been written about Botswana he is always referred to as being "immensely knowledgeable about Botswana and its people".

The first years of my life were spent in Serowe. Events began to register in my memory from about the age of three. One of the first of these was when I got into big trouble because my mother found me with a flit pump (old-fashioned insecticide pump before pressurised canisters were invented) trying to get a black mamba snake out of a hole in which it had sought refuge not long before. The black mamba is one of the deadliest snakes in the world and I don't think it would have been well disposed towards me had I succeeded in my endeavours.

From here on I have covered my life in the form of a series of stories which recall the various stages of my life. I also talk about my family and a number of members of the family, and I guess quite a lot more. Some of what I have written will interest my immediate family only but there are other parts which might have a broader appeal.

My Life by way of Thumbnail Express

1934
Serowe, Botswana. With my first cousins and brother and sister. I am on the extreme right aged two years. Dad was at that time District Commissioner.

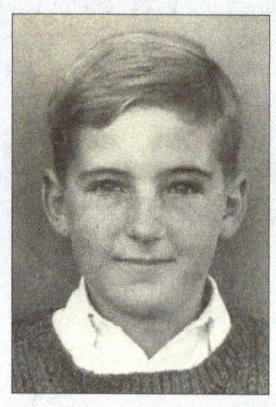

1944
Aged 12, attending school in Cape Town at Rondebosch Boys High. I was sent off to boarding school aged eleven. There were no suitable high schools in Botswana at that time.

1950
Dad dies aged fifty-six. In the picture, my mother is on the left and my sister on the right. Picture taken in 1948.

1952
Aged twenty, with my brother Gerald. A student at Cape Town University.

1953
Arrive in Lesotho and work in office of District Comissioner as an administrative assistant.

1954
British Government send me to Cambridge University for special studies appropriate to a career in the British Overseas Civil Service.

1956
District Officer, Maseru. Because I was still single I did frequent relieving duties in other districts in Lesotho.

1958
My brother Gerald trampled to death by an elephant when out shooting in Tanzania aged twenty-eight. He was at that time a District Officer in the British Colonial Service assigned to Tanzania.

1959
Seconded to British Diplomatic Service as Private Secretary to Sir John Maud, British High Commissioner to South Africa based in Cape Town, then Pretoria. I learnt a lot but did not really enjoy the diplomatic world.

1961
Appointed District Commissioner, Maseru, the senior district in Lesotho. Much political turbulence. I enjoyed the job.

1961
Marry Gail Turner. A good decision.

1962
Gail and I spend five months holiday — by sea up the African coast, Egypt, Lebanon, Turkey, Greece, Italy, UK, Ireland. Sea passages were paid for by the British Government. On full pay. Privileges for Colonial servants were generous. My leave entitlement was accumulated over a number of years.

1962
District Commissioner, Mokhotlong in Lesotho. Our house was at 8,000 feet up in the mountains. Three and a half wonderful years.

1965
Beverley born, our first child.

1966
Director of the Lesotho Independence Celebrations. Princess Marina represented the Queen. Forty-eight countries were represented by Presidents, Ambassadors etc. Huge crowds. Went off well.

1967
Awarded MBE. We went to see the Queen at Buckingham Palace! Not really, just another investiture.

1966
Tracy born on 23rd October at Pietermaritzburg, South Africa.

1967
Secretary to Chief Leabua Jonathan, Prime Minister of Lesotho. Travel abroad with him including visit to President Johnson at the White House where we stayed in Blair House.

1968
Director Food Aid Program in Lesotho, United Nations funded.

1969
Take my golden handshake in Lesotho and emigrate to Australia.

1970
Spend four wonderful months on Lord Howe Island. I was so relaxed that the effort of writing to my mother and posting it wore me out for the day.

1971
Build "Dandeloo", Coffin Bay. Served as our beach cottage for twenty-five years.

1970
Buy a house and settle in Adelaide. A happy house in Jellicoe Street, Linden Park.

1971
Penny is born at Calvary Hospital, Adelaide. Gail remarks – "In Lesotho I had three servants and no children. Now I have three children and no servants."

1973
Deputy State Director, Commonwealth Department of Aboriginal Affairs, South Australia. Stayed with the department for fifteen years. Later Director Aboriginal Housing for South Australia.

1975
Aged forty-three.
The hairy sideburns era! Fortunately it only lasted a year for me.

1977
Happy times at Dandeloo — our little bondwood boat "Sandpiper" served us well. We were very mediocre fishermen but still had great fun.

Three delightful daughters.

1984
My mother dies.

1984
Buy our eighty acres land near Clare and start the "Wuthering Heights" adventure.

1986
Plant 25,000 trees at "Wuthering Heights".

1989
Aged fifty-seven, retire from Dept. Aboriginal Affairs and work for TAFE for three years. Then private consulting for three years and in 1995 decide to devote my attention entirely to "Wuthering Heights".

1990
The weekend farmer.

1992
The mud brick house is finished.

1993
The Nettelton Family.

1994
We start our B&B business. This picture is of Glen Morris Cottage built in 1995 — the second cottage to be built.

1996
Gail dies aged sixty-two.

1995
Beverley marries Eivind Eikli, a Norwegian pilot she met in Botswana. Marriage was in St Marks Church, Bungaree, and the reception in a marquee at "Wuthering Heights".

1996 – 2002
On my own at "Wuthering Heights" with Molly and Patrick — my faithful dogs.

1998
Penny marries Jorn Gronset, a Norwegian pilot she met while working in Botswana. Wedding was in St Marks Church Bungaree and the reception in a marquee at "Wuthering Heights".

2000
The Bed and Breakfast business prospers. Picture shows entrance gates to "Wuthering Heights".

2002
Margie and I marry. Wedding was in Stirling, South Australia.

2004
Tracy marries Patrick in South Africa.

2018:

Still

going...

This is where my story begins
Memories of Serowe in the 1940s

Over a period of years our family had a strong presence in Serowe starting with the appointment of Grandad Nettelton as District Commissioner, Serowe, in 1922. Thereafter, Dad served for various periods, also as District Commissioner, between 1926 and 1942. My aunt, Madge Pagewood, my father's sister, married a Serowe trader and lived in Serowe until 1955 and my other aunt, Bimbi Ellenberger, was married to Vivien who also did time as District Commissioner there. My own clear recollections began in 1938 when Dad returned to Serowe as District Commissioner which was about the time the new DC's house was built, up on the hill overlooking the village, and soon after our arrival we moved in.

It was a big four-bedroomed house and the grounds were quite extensive. The hillside was quite rocky but that was no deterrent to a good garden because we had six prisoners who worked in it five days a week and Mum and Dad soon had the garden going, and by the time we left it really was a superb vegetable and flower garden. The house was surrounded by a barbed wire fence which kept the cattle out — there were many that came to graze in the vicinity belonging to local villagers.

I attended a little one-roomed school room which was exclusively for whites. We had a teacher who would have been in her late forties called Miss Barr. She had taught in Serowe for many years and I guess enjoyed the lifestyle and teaching in such a small group. The number of children in the class never exceeded eight. The schoolroom was not far from Dad's office and he used to drop me off at school in the morning on his way to work and then in the evening I somehow got back home finding a lift from one of the other parents — I don't quite remember.

My best friend was Gerald Cole who was the son of a local trader. He spoke very fluent Sechuana whereas I didn't. However I was academically bright and he struggled in class. One of my most vivid recollections of him was in the middle of prayers which Miss Barr always conducted at the beginning of the day. There was a rush of water at the back of the classroom where Gerald Cole was sitting and I well remember the little trickle of water coming down the floorboards and

Wonderful carefree days in an environment of wild birds and virgin bushland. I still treasure those days.

The Residency used by the District Commissioner until 1938. Elizabeth was born here.

The DC's office, Serowe.

Serowe Village, 1947

under my feet. The poor fellow had not been able to control his bladder in the middle of prayers. Funny how one remembers these awful things. On another occasion I remember in the middle of class his homemade ginger beer burst and splattered all around the room and Miss Barr was not pleased at all. On one occasion when Miss Barr was away on extended leave a very pretty young lady came to relieve her and I, at the tender age of seven or eight, was very impressed by this pretty lady and told Mum that I thought that I would fall in love with her. Miss Barr must have taught us well because when I went on to other schools in less remote areas, I was able to hold my own well.

Wanderings in the Veldt

After school I had time to wander the hills and valleys around the house. In those days the birdlife in the surrounds of Serowe was magnificent. I was very interested in birds and at a very tender age I knew *Roberts Birds of Southern Africa* almost backwards. I knew every single bird and there was a great variety of them. I collected nests, not eggs, and this collection was stored in a room at the back of the house but when we moved on to Mafeking in 1942 we didn't take it with us.

On occasions I went out with two little African herd boys and they showed me a lot about the berries and the edible bulbs. Serowe is on the fringes of the Kalahari Desert and would get a rainfall of about fifteen inches a year coming in the form of thunderstorms in the summer months. Despite the relatively low rainfall it is amazing what good groundcover there was and the savannah bushland was really prolific. I remember some of the names such as the Marula which was a delicious juicy fruit which grew on big trees. It has a leathery outer coat and a soft, sweet, fleshy interior with a pip. In February and March the Marula fruit drops off the tree and falls to the ground. A famous South African film produced by Jamie Uys brings in the Marula fruit because when it falls to the ground it ferments in its skin and the wildlife love to come and eat it but they get drunk, from the elephants down to the antelope. They roll all over the place and have terrible hangovers the next day. Jamie Uys was able to take some good film of the antics of drunken elephants, baboons and various antelope.

Then there was the Maretwa which was a little bush which, quite surprisingly for Botswana, had no thorns on it, and produced a reddy-orange fruit, quite small with a hard interior. These were quite sweet with a bit of pith around the hard interior. Birds love them. The Wag-n-bietjie bush produces an orange, fairly tart, fruit which I used to eat sometimes but not often — a bit too tart — but once again loved by the birds. The Wag-n-bietjie is so named because it is a very thorny bush and if your clothes come into contact you just wait and unhook yourself thorn by thorn and it takes time. Wag-n-bietjie in Afrikaans means 'wait a while'.

Then there was a wild potato which one learnt to dig out of the ground. It was edible raw with a lot of moisture in it. You chewed it and the taste was quite pleasant, and then generally you spat out the pith that you had chewed up.

My father gave me a pellet gun, or slug gun as they are called in Australia, for my seventh birthday and I'm not sure that it was a wise thing to do because I was a terrible slaughterer of birds. When I think back on it I am horrified at the way in which I used to go around shooting birds. One of the things which I remember vividly is shooting half a dozen doves in the afternoon; I would go back to the house and roast them with the prisoners. The hot water system for the house was based

The Marula tree.

on a forty-four-gallon drum which was built into a brick and cement structure enabling a fire to be built under the drum. Because of the elevation of the drum the water could then flow into the kitchen and the bathrooms.

The prisoners were always responsible for keeping the fire going and this resulted in a good layer of hot ashes and we used to simply throw the doves into the ashes without taking off feathers or cleaning out the insides. The feathers formed a charcoal coating and the bird cooked inside that. A dove doesn't have a great deal of flesh on it, you eat the breast and the two little drums and it is lovely meat. The prisoners certainly thought it was better than their normal prison diet!

The Haunted Residency

The new Residency at Serowe acquired the reputation for being haunted but this started after we had left Serowe. It was a new house so I don't know why it was haunted but my Aunt Madge, who claimed to be psychic, said that the house was built on an old bushman burial ground. We never had problems with the haunting aspect, although thinking back on it, I can remember walking down the passage at night on my own to go to bed and having a very strange feeling. The house did not have

New Residency built on the hill overlooking Serowe in 1938. We lived here from 1938 until 1942. Those who came after us swore that it was haunted — the bushmen spirits never worried us!

electric light, however, and we used pressure lamps and candles to light everything up. When I went to bed down that dark passage all I carried was a candle and I guess at the age of six, seven and eight it is a bit scary in a big house with dark passages and just a candle and you're taking yourself off to bed. The reason why I was going off on my own was that Gerald and Elizabeth, my elder siblings, had already left for boarding school.

The Ellenbergers and the MacKenzies were families who followed us to Serowe and lived in that house and both families had problems. The swing doors from the sitting room into the passage used to suddenly swing open despite the fact that there was no breeze coming through and in the night they used to hear the crashing of crockery in the pantry and have the feeling of someone leaning over and breathing. Both these families were very normal and not, one would think, at all prone to having worries about haunted houses but problems they had indeed. The Ellenbergers on occasions used to put stretchers out on the lawn and go and sleep outside. I don't know what the position is these days because the house is probably still there.

We Shot for the Pot

In those days, late 1930s and early 1940s, shopping facilities were very basic. There was a very primitive little butcher shop in Serowe where one could buy beef at "thruppence" per pound which would be equivalent to about 2.5 cents these days. As there was no refrigeration we used to buy some meat there but a lot of our meat came from our shooting expeditions. The game and bird life in the area was so prolific in those days that there was no problem at all in going out and shooting for the pot and keeping oneself in meat pretty constantly. We frequently went out

Guinea fowl.

to a place called Lewale which was about fifteen miles (24km) north of Serowe. Lewale had a lot of camelthorn trees and there was a dry riverbed that ran through the area and good grass cover. We used to shoot guinea fowl and francolin there. I was only eight when I first went out on one of these expeditions and by that stage I already owned a .22 rifle, a single-barrel 410 shotgun and a slug gun.

I used to shoot my share of guinea fowl and francolin and also sand grouse. One of the rules of the game was that you were never allowed to shoot a bird sitting on the ground: the bird must always be flying. Dad also put us through very rigorous safety training in the handling of guns. We were never allowed to get into a vehicle before we had unloaded our gun, or to go through or jump over a fence. We had to be extremely vigilant as to where the other members of the shooting parties were when firing a shot. Any departures from the rules led to some fairly drastic action by Dad and we soon learnt that you just did not break those rules.

Local Life

In those days the population of Serowe was no more than a couple of hundred whites and about 10,000 Africans who lived in the village itself. At Christmas time about six of the local trading families would close up their shops and their idea of a holiday was to go out to areas like Lewale and camp for about two weeks. It was hot at that time of the year but what they did was to send a contingent of their African employees out ahead and these were responsible for putting up the camp — they even used to make gravel croquet courts and temporary tennis courts, so they took their sport with them. We never went on these camps and I think it must have been pretty hot and quite dusty going out into those bush areas. I suspect that a lot of drinking was done. There was very little beer to be had because of the transport costs and most people drank spirits.

It was a real occasion for me to have a mineralised drink in those days and this treat was generally reserved for Sunday lunch. Sunday lunch, if we were at home and not out shooting, was a big affair. We ate huge amounts of meat and the vegetables were all supplied from our own garden. Temani, our cook, who stayed with us for thirty years, was a wonderful cook although he could not read or write and of course he did all the preparation and then everything was washed up by the kitchen boy. Mum needed only to read the ingredients of a recipe to him once and he never forgot them — a remarkable man and memory!

Although we had the prisoners to do the hard work in the garden, I none the less took a great interest in both Dad's vegetables and Mum's flowers and I'm sure that this is where my love of gardening started. As is so often the case with young people, I was like a sponge and I learned the names of all the flowers and vegetables and that has served me well to this day. I also took a great interest in the weather because rain was so important. From our position on top of the hill you could see storms approaching or going past and I used to watch with great interest the build-up of the big clouds which eventually turned into cumulonimbus with the big anvil at the top, and I always read the rain gauge with Dad.

In the spring there was the continual danger of locust swarms. The African locust is a lot bigger than the Australian counterpart and when they came over in their swarms they all but obscured the sun they were so thick. On two occasions I remember their coming across and we went out banging tins to try to keep them out of the garden but this had little success. The Africans eat the abdomen of the locust and regard it as a delicacy. I never found myself able to eat one. I guess it's rather similar to eating a witchetty grub. After a locust swarm had been through you could see the brown swathe across the countryside. It was as if a fire had gone through in the spring when everything was green and burnt off all the leaves. From the hilltop one could see this swathe right across the country.

Two of the fruits that I remember best at Serowe were cape gooseberries and pawpaws. We had three pawpaw trees and for six months of the year we had pawpaws. The fruit grew up the stem of the tree and the bottom one ripened first. You would pick that and then you would wait awhile and then the next one would be ripe and so on. Pawpaw for breakfast was one of my recollections of Serowe. The cape gooseberries grew in a bush which was about three feet high. They are orange with tiny seeds and make good eating and even better jam.

I always gardened with Mum or Dad and that is when I developed my love of gardening. I learnt so many names of both flowers and vegetables.

One of the tasks which I allotted to myself was keeping the big insects off the flowers and vegetables. There was a king-sized fellow which we called Stuttajohns and these big fat juicy things would be pulled off the vegetation and put on the ground, then you'd stamp on them. My mother told me that when we had previously lived in the old Residency in Serowe and I was very young, I used to pull the Stuttajohns off, stamp on them and then say "shame"!

There weren't many snakes but I do remember Dad shooting the occasional one. The birds were very good at advising one of the presence of snakes. They would get together in a noisy rabble above the snake and you could tell by the type of noise they were making that it was a "snake noise". Dad used his shotgun to shoot them when they came into the garden.

Scorpions

In those years the Second World War was in full swing and one of the war efforts which we indulged in was catching black scorpions and sending them to Pretoria in South Africa where the antivenene was made. At that time the troops were fighting in the North African Desert where there are an awful lot of scorpions and scorpion bites were quite a problem. The antivenene had been developed and in order to manufacture this, they needed a good supply of scorpions. The laboratories in Pretoria used to send us big flat boxes divided into about twelve compartments and you could open the lid of each compartment and put the scorpion in. We used to go traipsing over the hills with it

We collected scorpions during the war for the manufacture of antivenene.

and would generally take a couple of African servants with us, armed with crowbars and they would lever up the rocks and generally there would be a big black scorpion underneath. Dad used a pair of long flat tongs and he'd slide those underneath the carapace of the scorpion and get them into the box. We used to send dozens of black scorpions to Pretoria.

Sleeping Under the Stars in Lion Country

On occasions when the school holidays were on and Dad had to go out on a trip out into the district which entailed being away for some days, he used to take me along. The roads were just two tracks through the bush and one churned along at about ten or fifteen miles an hour, hour after hour, in a three-ton truck. No four-wheel drive in those days, no synchromesh gear box.

In the evening we would stop and we would build a half circle of thorn bush, quite thick, and our stretchers would be placed in the half moon and we would light a big fire at the foot of the beds. It was lion country and there were lots of them, also leopards and jackal and hyena. Along the way we would normally have shot either some birds or a stembuck or a springbok and we would feast on the fowl or a springbok steak cooked over the fire. The African cook normally came with us and there would be a camp attendant, so one was looked after well. We loved sitting round the fire and

Dad would tell his hunting stories. When in bed one would listen to the noise of the night. It was great to lie in bed and listen to the lions and hyenas and the ostriches and the jackals and all those noises of the night and the occasional awful noise when maybe a lion had pulled down a zebra. I never felt nervous. It was wonderful sleeping under the stars and I've never liked sleeping in a tent. In the morning Dad used to take us out and say that we were going to "read the newspaper", and that was to look at the spoors in the vicinity of the camp. On many an occasion there would be lion or hyena or jackal spoor not far from where we had slept. We were not exceptional. Those who knew the bush all did the same.

A Trip to Rakops with Dad 1945

On one occasion I went with Dad to a place called Rakops. It was a trip of about 250 miles along a sand track and it took us a day and a half to get there. Dad had to do a Court session and there were always the chiefs to talk to. Rakops had a small rest house which was for the exclusive use of the District Commissioner. I remember there were beautiful camelthorn trees there. I always took my pellet gun with me and also the rest of my armory but I was never allowed to use the .22 rifle or shotgun in areas where there might be people placed in danger. So when Dad was in Court I would take my pellet gun and go dove shooting. There were hundreds of the red-eyed doves, probably better to call them pigeons, which made a very mournful noise during the hot hours of the day. These doves were normally given to our attendants to eat and they loved them. We usually dined on bigger birds or venison.

Letlakane Desert track and troughs.

Letlakane Wells — As I Knew It in the 1940s

Halfway between Serowe and Rakops was a place called Letlakane Wells. At Letlakane there were wells going to a depth of about forty feet and the herdsmen would have a bucket on a chain and this would be on a well-rounded log with two spindles on each end so that they could wind the bucket up and down. The water was then poured into troughs made from hollowed-out tree trunks. There were a lot of cattle in the area and they were dependent on this water. The grazing was good but because of the sandy nature of the terrain, even when rain fell not much stayed on the surface for long. The herdsmen were almost entirely Basarwa Bushmen who were really in serfdom to the ruling African cattle owners. These areas were very remote and a number of the Basarwa were obviously of mixed parentage because of concubinage between the African cattle landlords and their employees.

Desert of Diamonds — In 1940 No One Knew It

Letlakane, 190km west of Serowe and right out in the middle of nowhere with those wells and those cattle, is today the site of one of the richest diamond mines in the world and a huge mining complex with modern houses owned by Debswana and De Beers Diamond Corporation.

Today: now site of one of the largest diamond mines in the world.

One of the strong recollections I have of those trips was the amount of game. On occasions the hartebeeste herds and the wildebeest herds and the springbok herds used to stretch in an unbroken swathe from one edge of the horizon to the other. There were literally tens of thousands of them. This was probably when there was a migration from one place to another following the good grazing. There was so much other game — it was everywhere. In 1969 when I went through that country again it was quite sad as to how little of that game remained. I feel privileged to have seen what the game of that area in a relatively undisturbed state looked like.

Wildebeeste populated the Letlakane area in the tens of thousands in the 1950s, along with herds of hartebeeste and springbok.

In our house at Serowe we had a lion's skin with the skull built into the skin and all the fearsome teeth showing and this lay on the floor in one of the living rooms. There was also a rhino horn which was a door stop. Both these were from Dad's early days in the 1920s in Ngamiland. He had on a certain occasion gone out shooting and had seen something which was partly obscured by a bush and thinking that it was a nice prospect for an evening meal he shot and soon discovered that he had wounded a rhino. The rhino took off into the bush and Dad and his tracker followed it. He went for quite a while and the wounded rhino did a semi-circle and came up behind him and charged him from about twenty yards. He was able to get behind a small tree and the rhino — rhinos have extremely poor vision — hit the tree and fell on its knees and Dad shot it. The next day he returned to take the rhino horn because in those days everyone was a trophy hunter; as he approached the rhino he saw the flick of a tail and a big black-maned lion pulled its head from inside the abdomen of the rhino which it had been eating. The lion was lying flat in the grass with the tail twitching, which was the obvious sign it was about to charge. Dad was a matter of only fifteen or twenty yards away and he shot the lion through the head, and that skin was the one which was on our floor. I shake my head when I think of that rhino horn and the fact that in the mid 1950s I can remember it being sent to the tip because it had become a bit weatherworn. Today the rhino is of course on the endangered list but on the black market it would sell for $30,000 to $40,000 to the medicine makers of China and some of the other South East Asian countries.

Caboose Trip to Tuli Block — 1950

In the mid-year university holidays of July 1950, I went on a trip in a caboose to the Tuli Block with Dad and Professor Isaac Schapera. Dad was Acting Resident Commissioner at this time. The powers that be still had him "acting" after 18 months! He had taken the full brunt of the Seretse Khama affair (described later in this memoirs) over the past year and he was tired and unwell.

Nonetheless, he insisted that he arrange an official trip into Botswana to coincide with the university holidays so that Gerald and I could go along as well as Professor Schapera, an old friend, who was also Gerald's and my Social Anthropology lecturer at Cape Town University.

We travelled in a caboose, accompanied by a one-tonne pick-up.

The caboose was a ten-tonne monster seating driver and two passengers in front seat, with four passengers in the cab behind the driver. Then came the accommodation cabin with four bunks, small hanging wardrobe and four drawers. Squeezed in was a small wash basin. At the rear end of the vehicle was a good storage tray. A lot of the space was taken up by drums of petrol.

A caboose is not a vehicle for speed. We left Mafeking in the morning and camped that night close to the Macloutsi (Motloutse) River in the Tuli Block, a journey of less than 300 kilometres. The weather was glorious, and rather than use the bunks in the caboose we slept under the stars after

A caboose, a ten-tonne monster designed to accommodate senior officials in comfort on trips made to remote areas.

Our campsite in the Tuli Block, close to the Macloutsi River.

a meal eaten around the camp fire. We had a cook, two drivers and a camp attendant with us so we were well looked after.

Early next morning Gerald and I went out shooting, and Gerald got a good kudu bull. I missed a warthog at point-blank range! Gerald and I had commandeered the pick-up and Dad was fetched from our bush camp by the police officer in charge of the area and taken to the official government complex some miles away: a collection of houses, an office and a whole lot of thatched rondavels.

It was very obvious that in true colonial style everything had been given a fresh coat of whitewash in honour of the visit. The joke that everyone abided by was that when a senior official paid a visit, the locals whitewashed all the immovables and saluted anything that moved.

A visit to the area by the Resident Commissioner was a major event for local officialdom with a police guard of honour and the police officer's wife dressed in her best finery, complete with hat and handbag. A poor lady in her isolation would not have had too many occasions to dress up.

As misfortune would have it, Gerald and I pitched up in the middle of proceedings with a kudu bull half dangling out of the pick-up and pouring blood all over the place. (It was of course very dead but still recently enough deceased for the blood to run freely.) It really was very embarrassing. Dad took it well but in hindsight the two of us really did deserve a dressing down.

Track across the Macloutsi River, Tuli Block. The Macloutsi is a dry river bed most of the year but must have an underground stream because it is heavily foliaged on either side by both large and small trees. There is lots of wildlife – kudu, wild pig, stembuck, duiker and guineafowl.

In addition to the caboose, we had a one-tonne pickup truck as an escort.

Siblings and Cousins

Gerald, my brother, was sent off to boarding school at the age of nine. He went to Rondebosch Boys High in Cape Town which was well over one thousand miles away and only came home for six weeks at Christmas and four weeks in the mid year. I went to boarding school when I was eleven. My sister Elizabeth went to boarding school when she was ten. I hardly knew my sister because I was only six when she went. The posh school in Johannesburg she went to was a three-term school and I went to a four-term school and so the only time that we saw one another was for six weeks at Christmas time. It must have been very hard on my parents to have all three children at boarding school by the time I was eleven and for them only to see us for so short a time during the year. However, looking at the three of us, it didn't seem to do us too much harm because we all did well and were pretty well balanced.

Crimson-breasted shrike.

We moved from Serowe to Mafeking when Dad was promoted to the position of Government Secretary, the second most senior official in the country, in 1942. One of the things I'm glad about is that before leaving Serowe I had given up shooting birds. It's a strange thing but I have a vivid recollection of an occasion when I shot a crimson-breasted shrike, which is a beautiful bird, and as it lay on the ground, its partner came and sat on it and tried to revive it. It made such an impression on me that I didn't use my pellet gun again after that.

Those years in Serowe were good from a family point of view because I got to know my first cousins. We were fortunate in that Dad's sister, Madge Pagewood, was living in Serowe. She married Uncle Kissy, Alfred Pagewood, who was a well-to-do trader in Serowe. They had three children, Andrew, Marigold and Geoffrey, born in 1926, 1931 and 1938 respectively. Then there was the Ellenberger family. Bimbi, the youngest in Dad's family, married Vivien Ellenberger, a District Commissioner. When we were in Serowe the Ellenbergers were living in Gaberone where Uncle Vivien was the District Commissioner. They had two children, Peter and Felicité. It was not all plain sailing because I have recollections of great tensions between Madge and Bimbi and on occasion Dad having to mediate between the two. They just didn't seem to get on well together and looking back on it I better understand the reason for the disagreements, because Bimbi and Madge were sisters of very different temperament.

All the cousins were sent off to boarding school at quite a young age. Andrew Pagewood went to Bishops Diocesan College in Cape Town, an expensive and leading school in South Africa. Marigold Pagewood went to Herschel Girls Collegiate in Cape Town, also one of the expensive and well known girls' private schools in South Africa. Geoffrey Pagewood went to St John's College in Johannesburg, an English and Anglican private school of some considerable status. Peter Ellenberger, Gerald my brother and myself all went to Rondebosch Boys High in Cape Town, a well known and very much respected semi-Government school. By semi-Government I mean that although it was classified a Government school, fees were charged. Felicité Ellenberger went to Wynberg Girls High.

Adults from left:
Mum, Madge, Granny Nettelton
(seated) and Bimbi.
Children: Marygold, Gerald,
Peter, me (on Granny's lap)
Michael Pagewood and Felicité.

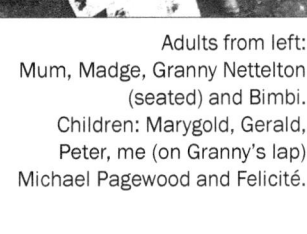

Elizabeth and Gerald.

My Cousins in Serowe — 1934

L-R: Peter Ellenberger, Andrew Pagewood, Elizabeth Nettelton, Felicité, Gerald, Marygold, Spencer Nettelton. My doll was called 'Twinkle Toes'.

L-R: Felicité, Peter Ellenberger, Gerald Nettelton, Andrew Pagewood, Marygold Pagewood, Elizabeth Nettelton, Spencer Nettelton.

Social Life

As cousins we met mainly during the school holidays and our meetings always seemed to be associated with sporting or shooting events. Serowe had a very active tennis and croquet club. The parents participated over weekends mainly. There was also a golf course which was quite rough and had gravel greens. The children went with their parents to the Saturday afternoon tennis and croquet parties at the local Europeans only club. All our parents were keen on sport. Dad and Madge were good all-round sports people. Mum played tennis in a very social sort of sense.

Dad, Gerald Nettelton.

One of the games which was often played by us children was called "coo-ee". The game consisted of two teams and you threw a tennis ball over the roof of a shed behind the tennis club and the team on the other side had to catch the ball and if they did, they tore around the corner and tried to tag a member of the opposing side by throwing the tennis ball at them and trying to hit them. The closer you could get and the harder you could throw it and the more it hurt, the better the game. So you had these two teams tearing around and around the shed, throwing balls over the top and trying to tag one another with the ball. These games could go on for ages.

The eats at these functions were always superb. Everyone would bring a cake and probably a plate of sandwiches and scones and all sorts of things. We ate sumptuously; I guess the fact that there were servants who knew how to cook and who would do all the washing up afterwards made life in that respect quite easy. My recollections are that we had huge amounts because not only did we have the main evening meal, which was always meat and at least three vegetables and a pudding, but we also had a big midday meal, very often cooked. Something like a macaroni cheese, or a shepherds pie or something in that nature would be served up at lunch time. The breakfast was normally cooked and it always consisted of a plate of porridge plus sausages and egg or a piece of steak and egg plus toast and coffee or tea or a glass of milk.

Many kept their own cow and so one drank lots of milk, unpasteurised and full of cream, from one's own cow. In many ways we were pretty self sufficient because a lot of the meat we shot, the vegetables we grew, we kept our own cows, the bread was always made by the cook, jams frequently were made from one's own produce, the cordial was from lemons from one's own lemon tree and so it went on. Provisions could be bought from the local trading stores but their stock was mainly orientated towards the big African population whose requirements were not always similar to those of the whites. Mum used to order a case of groceries every so often from Mafeking down south and this came up on the railway and was then brought across from Palapye Road by a local transport lorry.

Brutus

We had at that time a dog called Brutus, a sort of fox terrier who had been owned by Dad before he got married but had integrated quite well into the family. He was good with the children. I can remember having many battles with Brutus in the back seat because Brutus always wanted to have his head out of the window and I wanted that seat. There were occasions when Brutus would be leaning out of the window and on those very twisty dirt roads a sudden veer to one side by the car would see him shoot out the window, but this didn't seem to perturb him — you would look back and there he would be, rolling over in the dust, then he would get up and start running after the car. It was a source of annoyance to me that when there were smells in the car the conversation always was as to whether that smell emanated from me or Brutus. I always felt that discrimination against me, being the youngest in the family and therefore I was the one most likely to have farted. I'm quite certain it was often Gerald but he never seemed to get the blame.

Brutus enjoyed going out into the veldt with Gerald and me when we had our pellet gun and were shooting birds.

We had one nasty accident. We had a new Chev car which we got about 1939 and on one occasion when Mum was driving, a tie was about to fly out the window; Mum tried to grab the tie and was not looking at the road so Dad grabbed the steering wheel and pulled it over. It caught a lip on the road and over the car went. It turned over three times. We were fortunate that there were no real injuries. I had quite a nasty cut at the base of my thumb which was caused by the sight of Dad's rifle which was lying on the seat next to me, and I still have the scar.

Left: Dad and Brutus, 1926.

Brutus, the fox terrier of mixed origins, was a family favourite.

Royal Visit to Basutoland, Botswana, Swaziland and South Africa 1947

The background to this royal tour to southern Africa is as follows: During WWII, the South African Prime Minister, General Smuts, formed a close relationship with Winston Churchill, Prime Minister of the United Kingdom. Apparently, Churchill thought very highly of Smuts. General Smuts no doubt felt that with hostilities easing and a return to normal politics between nations soon to resume, it would be a good time to advance the desires of South Africa to incorporate Basutoland, Bechuanaland and Swaziland into South Africa in accordance with what Smuts felt would be a sensible and always envisaged outcome.

This was by no means the purpose of the Royal Tour but the incorporation issue was certainly on the political agenda. The marriage of Chief Sir Seretse Khama to Ruth Williams that took place in 1948 brought with it a huge complication to a smooth incorporation process. How was apartheid South Africa going to deal with the fact that the most senior chief in South Africa was now married to a white woman, a marital arrangement that would in South Africa be illegal? This issue caused big ructions in South Africa, Bechuanaland and in Whitehall, London. I have written about the Seretse and Ruth issue in detail in Volume 4 of these memoirs. Dad, as senior functional administrator on the ground in Botswana, had to deal with this issue. It was not easy. But with that background explanation out of the way, what about the Royal Tour?

Dad played a prominent role in hosting the royal family as can be seen in the accompanying photograph. The visit of the royals went off smoothly and was well supported by both black and

L-R: Dad (Gerald Nettelton, Queen Elizabeth, Princess Margaret, King George.

white citizens. The South African segment of the royal tour went off equally well. I was at that time at boarding school in Cape Town. There was still a royal fervour amongst the main segment of the South African white community and there were huge crowds wherever the royals went.

Looking back at that era, in South African theatres and public functions, *God Save the Queen* was always played before the function commenced. When the Afrikaans-dominated party won the parliamentary elections in the late 1940s the loyalties began to wane and *God Save the Queen* ceased to be played at public functions.

The Ossewa Brandwag (ox wagons around the campfire) organisation, which was anti-British and had pro-German elements within it, was allowed a lot of freedom by the new nationalist Afrikaaner government. At the time of the royal tour the controversy surrounding Princess Margaret and wing commander Peter Townsend was on the boil. It was becoming apparent that the marriage to Townsend desired by Margaret was going to be blocked and Mum and Dad found Princess Margaret very sullen when the royal party visited Bechuanaland. Poor girl! I always felt Princess Margaret never really found happiness. She was a lively spirit caged in by royal prerogative.

She was a very beautiful woman — those deep, deep blue eyes and perfect peaches and cream skin had to be admired.

The visit to Bechuanaland went off extremely well and the royal party certainly enhanced respect for themselves by the way they conducted themselves in such a friendly, relaxed manner.

Tshekedi Khama, Regent of the Bamangwato tribe in Botswana. In this picture he is accompanied by my father, Gerald Nettelton, and Sir Arden Clarke, Resident Commissioner of Botswana at that time. Seretse Khama was still a minor.

Tshekedi Khama of the Bamangwato

At that time Tshekedi Khama was the Regent for the Bamangwato tribe whose capital was at Serowe. He was a well-educated and cultured man and I remember him well. On occasions Dad took me with him when he went to see Chief Tshekedi. He was always polite and well-mannered but he was a very tough and resolute politician who had an excellent perspective on the wider world. He opposed mineral development on the basis that the day would come when the people of Bechuanaland would control their own resources and the money from mining would go to his own people and not to the Colonialists. He was able to say this in a manner which was not offensive. Of course this attitude was not well liked by the British Government hierarchy who saw the Colonies as places from which the wealth that flowed to England emanated. Tshekedi's predictions came true because later very rich diamond fields were found and Orapa is now one of the richest diamond mines in the world, and there are also rich deposits of potash, copper and coal that are mined. In fact, Bechuanaland has moved to a situation in the present day where it is regarded as the Switzerland of Africa. Not bad going when you consider that fifty years ago it was regarded as one of the poorest countries, not only in Africa but in the world. One of the big factors in this success has been political stability. This is attributable to a number of factors. Enlightened leadership from the Chieftainship which was well educated, the fact that there has never been a land problem in Botswana because a country as big as France has a population of just over a million people, so there has not been pressure on the land, and also Botswana was lucky in having a succession of good administrators who laid a great foundation for future success. Dad was one of those people.

Seretse and Ruth in Serowe 1948.
(In 2016 a film of the story, *United Kingdom*, starring David Oyelowo and Rosamund Pike, was released.)

Seretse Khama Affair 1948–1950

I have written in some detail about this matter because it so intimately involved Dad. The detailed story of the relationship between the Netteltons and the Khamas over four generations can be found in Volume III. I did, however, want to make some reference it in this volume, so the brief summary of what occurred is as follows.

In the mid-1940s Seretse Khama was studying for a law degree at Oxford University when he met Ruth Williams, an English girl. He advised his uncle, Chief Tshekedi Khama, of his intentions toward Ruth. Tshekedi was at that time acting as Regent pending Seretse's completion of his university studies, when he would be of an age where he could take over his traditional role as Chief of the Bamangwato people. There was considerable displeasure on behalf of Tshekedi Khama, while the British Government also felt it would be inappropriate. The British Government had in mind the complications it would cause for Botswana in its relations with apartheid South Africa.

Seretse went ahead and got married and then followed a long tussle as to when he might take over his role as Chief of the Bamangwato. Dad was very much in the forefront of the long-drawn-out negotiations as to what should best be done to resolve the matter. After two years the British Government appointed a judicial commission to report on what they considered to be the best line of action. Dad was one of the three on the judicial commission. The ultimate recommendation of the commission, which one suspects was predetermined at the will of the British Government, was that

Seretse as a boy in Serowe, 1923.

Ruth with baby Jacqueline, 1949

Seretse should be banished from Botswana.

This matter attracted worldwide attention. The stress of two years in the forefront of protracted discussions, which at times were quite acrimonious, had adverse effects on Dad's health and he died on 11 August 1950, which ironically was the very day on which Ruth and Seretse departed Botswana for the UK to serve out an initial five-year exile. Ultimately Seretse returned to Botswana, relinquished his traditional position as Chief of the Bamangwato, entered politics and became Botswana's first President, a position which he fulfilled with great dignity and huge success. The marriage of Seretse and Ruth turned out to be a real success story and Lady Ruth became a very much respected and dignified President's wife. Seretse died prematurely of a kidney disease when in his late 50s. His son Ian some years later became President and once again is serving with success. One of the redeeming features of Botswana is that although the country has became wealthy it is not plagued by corruption amongst the political elite and I believe this is due to the fact that Seretse set down very definite rules of behaviour and these have been retained right up until the present.

Seretse Khama Affair Postscript

Letter written by Dad to my mother not long before he died

A letter from Dad written in November 1949 to my mother provides a personal backdrop to what was going on in Dad's personal life when he was sitting on the Seretse Khama Judicial Commission late in 1949. Eight months later Dad died.

The Commission was much criticised in subsequent years for its recommendations. The British Government in the latter stages of the Commission's deliberations almost certainly instructed them as to what their findings must be. Pressure from the South African Government was the main factor.

Serowe
16/11/49

My Dearest Helen,

Tomorrow is our wedding anniversary and it is the first one we have spent away from one another. I suppose our lives undergo changes. I sit in the Commission tent – I look across at the room in which Elizabeth was born nearly 22 years ago – and it looks so shabby and it now has a vegetable garden in front – quite sensible. I hope tomorrow brings to you no great regrets – it does not to me. In fact my one wish is to be home again and I send you all my love. It began raining at 5 am and looks as if it will rain on and off for days. It hinders us as 98% of the audience do not hear the very soft spoken witnesses let alone with noise of the rain on the tent. I am afraid we will be here another week at this rate: Seretse's witnesses are so suspicious that even Fracukel (their lawyer) has given one of them best. Everyone is of course waiting for Seretse's evidence. He has had some harsh things to listen to since we began.

Dad, Gerald Nettelton

The Sullivans had a huge sundowner party last night to which they asked every European except Ruth: I went for a while.

Things are grim. My mother had a bad heart attack yesterday. I say it was because of the quarrelling of her daughters. It was all rather dreadful and I have had to read the riot act. (This is for you only). That is why we have asked Tommy Quigley to come and nurse my mother. Madge is worn out and not very responsible for what she says. Bimbi is not prepared to put herself out to help and one seldom sees Felicity. The atmosphere is charged and together with the pressures of my Commission work things are hard, but it will no doubt all work itself out. My mother is very weak and it would be a blessing for the end to come and that's what she wants but she remains very cheerful. Another violent heart attack and retching early this morning. When she can be moved she will be transferred to hospital. She's willing to go. She relies a lot on Madge. There is the dreadful jealousy between Madge and Bimbi and it is incomprehensible why it should come up at this juncture.

We have just done our morning session with Seretse giving evidence. One can't say how long it will last.

My thoughts will be with you tomorrow. We grow old but we go along quite happily and one day we too will be dead.

With all my love,

Ever Yours, Gerald

Mafeking Stad, 1992

The Minchin house, Mafeking, 1992

Mafeking – A Victorian Legend

I think Brian Gardner explains the background well in the following preface to his book *Mafeking, A Victorian Legend* which I'd like to use as an introduction to the town with which my family has had a strong connection for more than a century.

"The idea of writing this book [*Mafeking, A Victorian Legend*] was twofold: first, to tell the story of a famous military drama; second, to investigate why that event was so important to its generation — for the relief of Mafeking brought a greater national communion than any similar occasion in British history until that time. The former had been done before, but without much attention being paid to the latter, the answer to which, as might have been expected, was found more in the final eddies of the Victorian Age in Britain than in Mafeking itself. As for the military drama, I discovered before I even began to write that the facts did not always support the legend."

He goes on: "[The 19th century had been] the age of the Great Queen. People of all colours, religions and races, who lived on more than a quarter of the earth's surface, owed allegiance to the grumpy, Germanic monarch of the island off the coast of Europe. Britain was at the peak of her power. Her sons were administrators and merchants and lawyers and missionaries in every part of the globe. Her technical skill and her industrial might, dating from her early start in the industrial revolution, were acknowledged by all. Her Navy was the mightiest and most feared instrument of power in the world. Her people were proud."

The people of Britain, most of whom lived monotonous lives in poor housing and had humdrum jobs, took huge pride and interest in the exploits of British armies and stories relating to the mysteries of the East and other British colonies. Uprising and revolts against anything British were severely suppressed using the might of the British navy and military. Britain had little knowledge of defeat.

In the late 19th century Britain sought to extend its interests northwards. It had an unlimited lust for more gold and diamond resources. But then it came up against two small, insignificant Boer republics — the Transvaal and the Orange Free State Republics, who resisted the British political and financial incursions into territory they regarded as their own. The British armed forces sent out to subdue the Boers found themselves up against white men who knew the landscape intimately, were well armed using German 7mm Mauser rifles which they used with deadly accuracy, and who fought by way of small guerrilla groups, highly mobile. The Boers actually inflicted some defeats on the British and their efforts to subdue the Boers were not getting anywhere. The situation was humiliating to the British; what was psychologically needed was a British success. And finally it got one. After nine months during which Mafeking was totally surrounded, the Boer forces withdrew. The previously totally unknown and insignificant town of Mafeking became a centrepiece of interest throughout the British Empire. In Britain, the rejoicing was at a level never seen before. That was the night the word Mafik ("to rejoice") was invented and a hundred years later it still appears in most dictionaries.

Both my mother and my father were in Mafeking for the full duration of the siege and my aunt was born during the siege.

Early School Days in Mafeking, 1942-1944

In 1942 Dad was promoted to the position of Government Secretary, the second most senior position in the Bechuanaland Government, and we moved to Mafeking.

The house we lived in had no neighbours and there was a fair bit of bushland around through which I used to wander. On one occasion a meerkat got in and attacked one of my hens and I ran inside and got my 410 shotgun and shot it as it ran out into the bush near the fowl run. It was so undeveloped in those days that there were still wild animals adjacent to the property. On a couple of occasions there were snakes. Fowls are good at killing snakes so long as they are small ones and then they eat them. Amongst the fowls the bantam cock was always king of the roost. The bantam cock was always out to fight one of those big lumbering black ostrolop or white leghorn cocks. The bantam cock would mate with other fowls and the cross breeds that resulted were quite interesting.

I used to ride my bicycle to school at the Mafeking Convent which was right out on the other side of town. Of course it was not a very big town but Mafeking in those days was an important railway centre. It was the junction for the railway line which came from Johannesburg across to Mafeking and then up to Rhodesia, and also the other lines which came from the south, from places such as Cape Town, Port Elizabeth, etc. There was a great deal of development going on in Rhodesia, Northern Rhodesia and further north. Many trains came through and in those days all the engines were steam engines.

I had to ride through what was known as the Railway Camp which was the housing area for the staff who worked on South African Railways. They were mainly Afrikaans and went to Mafeking High School which we regarded as being a pretty rough high school. There was still that residue of hate between Afrikaner and English which had its origins in the Boer War where the British were pretty ruthless in the manner in which they finally won and subdued the Afrikaners, who were really the first exponents of guerrilla warfare which they did very successfully. When I rode through the Railway Camp I occasionally had stones thrown at me and for a little boy of eleven, who couldn't speak Afrikaans and on his own on his bicycle, it was quite frightening. Sometimes I would not have the courage to do the ride through the Railway Camp and I would go via the main road which was a long way round.

At the Mafeking Convent I was taught by Sister Ita. In those days the nuns wore their complete habit and it must have been very hot in summer. The Principal of the Convent was Sister DeSales who had been there for many years. Sister Ita was quite fierce and Sister DeSales very nice, but firm. Sister Ita taught the standard fives and sixes in one class and there would have been about twenty-five of us in all. I had no difficulty with my lessons and was still at that stage where my memory was almost photographic. One of my recollections is reading the Ten Commandments and being able to recite them to Mum and Dad word for word after one reading. They were most impressed. I wish my memory was still as good as it was in those days.

The Convent had a big playground just across the road which was used as a soccer field and there were two tennis courts. One of my worst recollections was when I was beaten at tennis by Patsy Lorensen. I was supposed to be quite a good player and on that day I just couldn't hit the ball properly and Patsy, a pretty blonde girl of about my own age, beat me. Patsy was the daughter of Mum's bridesmaid and of course there was a lot of talk about this tennis match which had resulted in a win for the gentler sex. It hurt my male pride greatly.

Another recollection I have is a fist fight that I somehow got into during one of our lunch breaks. I cannot imagine how it all happened because I wasn't an aggressive child. I can only think that my peer group egged me on. I approached my adversary, Gerald Gordon, son of the local butcher, with my fists clenched but hanging round my waist. He didn't hesitate and hit me one solid punch in the eye and that was the end of it. I had a black eye and I didn't have the courage to talk to my parents about it and they never mentioned it, but it was fairly humiliating.

Mafeking Recreation

We had now entered the era of a more town-oriented style of life and we were unable to go on weekend shooting trips as frequently as we had done when living at Serowe. However that didn't mean that we never went at all. In Mafeking we were twenty miles south of the Bechuanaland Protectorate border and during the duck-shooting season, which was November to March — and provided there had been some rain in Botswana to fill the pans with water — we would go out shooting on a Sunday. The usual procedure was that we went to 7.30 Communion at the Anglican Church, where Dad was Church Warden, and as soon as the service was over, we would dash home, get into our shooting gear and make tracks for the duck-shooting pans. These pans were depressions which collected water after heavy rains because there was no outlet for the water to escape and with the clayey bottoms, the water didn't sink into the ground. There was usually quite good grass growth in the water and the duck like this. We would walk into the water with our shot guns and put up the duck which often would circle and come back over you and you'd try to bring them down.

One of the hazards of these pans was leeches. When you stood in the water for more than a minute or so you would look down and your ankles would be covered with black leeches, wriggling their bottoms in delight as they sucked your blood. Once they got a hold on you they were very difficult to get off and when you did you bled quite a lot. To prevent the bleeding one of the easiest ways was to put a lit cigarette on their bottoms and they let go in a hurry. Another aspect of such trips was that in summer there were a lot of ticks which could be picked up walking through grass.

These ticks were of various varieties, some very tiny and others quite big. When we got home in the tick season Mum used to insist that we got into a bath which had Dettol in it and she would also do a good inspection to make sure that the tiny ticks hadn't got into our hair or various cleavages on the body.

One of the brightest moments of my duck-shooting career in that era was when I shot a Spur Winged Goose at two hundred yards with my single-shot Remington .22 rifle and the bullet went right through its heart. I reckoned it was a pretty good shot but in actual fact it was a fluke. Spur Winged Geese are not easy to bring down with a shotgun. They are not good eating, being very tough. We also got Egyptian Geese which is a smaller brown bird, and these fly with a honking noise, quite attractive. They are good eating. The main duck that we shot were the Red Billed Teal and the Yellow Billed Teal. They are really good eating. They fly quite fast and are not always easy to bring down, particularly if they are coming past flying with the wind. They can get up quite a turn of speed. Dad and Gerald were excellent bird shots. I was okay but they were much better than I was. On these expeditions sometimes the women came with us and sometimes they didn't. They didn't shoot so it would have been a bit boring for them sitting around waiting for us to come back, but on some occasions they did come along. We seldom stayed overnight.

Proud catch of a Spur Winged Goose.

One of the recreation places out of town that we went to most frequently was the Wondergat. This was on a private farm which we were allowed to visit. The Wondergat was a round, very, very deep sink hole about two hundred yards across with high precipitous rock cliffs on all sides apart from one place where one could get down to the water. It was beautiful clean water and we enjoyed swimming there because there weren't often many people around. We also used to do a bit of fishing for Barbel, which are not good eating because they taste very muddy. I used to enjoy those days that we went out to the Wondergat because the whole family and probably a couple of other families would go along together. There were lots of nice trees and we'd have lunch and probably a barbecue and there would be a lot of swimming, and we also used to take inflated motor car tyre tubes which we were able to float in and this was good fun.

Rooigrond was another place we used to go to. It was not far out of Mafeking and there was a hotel there with a swimming pool. In those days very few houses had their own swimming pools and we never went to the swimming bath in the Railway Camp, we were too scared to. There was no public swimming pool in Mafeking until many years later. So being able to have a swim was really quite a luxury in Mafeking in those days.

Another place we occasionally went to was the Gubbins' farm about thirty miles from Mafeking. This was owned by Elizabeth Gubbins who had inherited it from her father. She did not marry until quite late in life. She married a Mr Rose who was an engineer from West Africa and who tragically died only a few years after their marriage. Elizabeth rather went to pieces after that. In later years I remember going to lunch at the Gubbins' farmhouse accompanied by Spencer Minchin and various others and by the end of the luncheon Elizabeth was always pretty tiddly. The Gubbins' farm had its days of glory when Mr Gubbins was a wealthy entrepreneur and also a man of considerable anthropological knowledge. He accumulated an impressive array of English and Dutch antiques. The Gubbins' house was a veritable museum. In the lounge was an old English water clock which was dated to 1595 and must have been priceless. One of the tragedies was that he had stored quite a lot of his Afrikaner antique furniture in a warehouse in Johannesburg because he couldn't accommodate it at the farm and the warehouse burnt down. That would have been in the late 1930s. It was a real tragedy.

On the Gubbins' farm there was a natural spring which flowed out of the rock and formed a veritable fast-running river across their farm. The water was of beautiful quality and even in those days in the 1940s I believe the

Spencer Nettelton revisits the Wondergat in 1992.

Gubbins had been offered half a million pounds by the Mafeking Municipality for part access to the water. The Gubbins refused. They did not seem to do a great deal with that water but they didn't need the money anyway. When Elizabeth Gubbins was widowed and lived on her own she was obviously very lonely and she had this considerable wealth and just no family at all to pass it on to. One of the really bizarre things was that she approached Spencer and Connie Minchin, who at that stage had four children ranging in age from four to twelve, and asked whether it would be possible to adopt Peter, who at that stage was eight years old. She had previously taken Peter, naturally with the permission of his parents, on a four-week overseas trip with all expenses paid. Peter was quite a rebellious young man but Elizabeth seemed to find him most appealing. Naturally Spencer and Connie very firmly refused to allow their second son to be taken over by Elizabeth. Connie never liked Elizabeth and after that I think it went even deeper. Elizabeth always fancied Spencer Minchin.

One of the entertainments in Mafeking was the Bioscope. It was one of those old-fashioned places with hard seats and a seating capacity of probably about two hundred. On one occasion I went to a matinee which included something about Red Riding Hood and, not being used to the cinema, the wolf really frightened me. The cinema was dark and I can't remember who I was with but I quietly got up and went outside because I couldn't take any more. On another occasion when I was seeing a film with my parents, when a certain gentleman was being really nasty to the heroine, an Afrikaans guy somewhere up in the front seats stood up and held his hands in front of him and he was shaking and he said in Afrikaans "As ek my hande on sy nek kan kry" — if I could just get my hands round his throat. Then he realised where he was and sat down quickly, no doubt very embarrassed. As children we paid sixpence to get into the cinema. Mum and Dad paid two shillings each.

With Dad a senior officer in the British Colonial Service, my parents had to do a lot of entertaining. There were frequent cocktail parties and dinner parties and at a very early age we were encouraged to help hand round eats and I also helped my mother and at times Temani in preparing snacks for cocktail parties. It stood me in very good stead because during my bachelor days I could always turn on a really good array of snacks when I had in turn, as a District Commissioner, to entertain.

In 1944 at age eleven I went off to boarding school in Cape Town.

Mafeking and My Family

Our family's long association with Mafeking stretched from 1890 until 2013. Incidentally, the correct spelling of Mafeking is in fact Mafikeng, meaning "the place of rocks" in the language of the Barolong tribe in whose country the town is located. While Mafikeng is the spelling of choice now, during my time in Africa the historical British spelling of Mafeking was in use and I have opted to keep it throughout this memoir in preference to swapping from one spelling to the other depending on context.

Before I enlarge on my own family connection to the town I will give a short historical outline of the black-white conflicts from 1850 onwards.

European intrusion onto Barolong tribal land began in the 1850s, mainly by Afrikaner Boers moving up from the south in quest of new lands upon which to settle, and this inevitably led to conflict. In 1854 two mini Boer republics were declared: Goshen located at Rooigrond and Stella-land at Vryburg. Rooigrand is of particular interest to me because it is located fifteen kilometres south of Mafeking and in my school and university days it had a hotel with a big swimming pool which was the one pool in the whole area open to the public. Dad used to sometimes take us there for a swim on hot days as Mafeking could get very hot in summer.

To cut a long story short, there was eventually British intervention and the two Boer mini republics were abandoned and the fighting ceased, but this did not restore all the land back to the Barolong tribe — only some of it, with the majority eventually taken over by white farmers.

My grandfather on my mother's side was born to British parents living at the time in Madras (now Chennai) in India where his father worked for the East India Company in a senior legal position. Grandad was sent back to London to study law at Lincoln's Inn where he qualified in the late 1880s. He came from an upper class family with what is snobbishly called "good connections".

He was on his way back to India to take up what would have been a "suitable" legal job with The East India Company but on the voyage met a man who owned a wholesale business in Mafeking. He persuaded Grandad that South Africa was the country for a young aspiring lawyer, what with the discovery of gold and diamond prospects that were generating great wealth and expansion. What more would a young, single lawyer want? And Mafeking was a town in an area with great prospects and without a lawyer. So Grandad abandoned his return to India and set off for Mafeking where he set up his legal practice in the name of "Minchin and Kelly" which for the next 140 years always employed at least one Minchin lawyer. Grandad would have travelled by train from Cape Town, where he disembarked at Mafeking. The railway had by then passed northwards through Mafeking, funded mainly by Cecil Rhodes, the diamond/gold billionaire who was pursuing his dream of a Cape Town to Cairo railway with all the country on the way coloured red on the map; in other words, governed by Britain. Writing the last sentence suddenly took my memory back to the Rhodes memorial on the slopes of Table Mountain. I knew that memorial well in my university days; it was quite isolated with a lovely view over the Cape Flats with the Hottentots Holland Mountains in the distance as a backdrop. The inscription on the memorial was this:

"I dreamed my dream of country to Northwards
Aye one land
From Lions Head to Lion."

"Lions Head" was Cape Town and "Lion" was Egypt. It was called Rhodes' "Cape to Cairo" dream. When Rhodes was premier of the Cape Colony in the 1880s and 1890s, my great-uncle George Paton, who was the parliamentary member for the Barkly West area, was his Treasurer for eight years (see George Paton in Volume III of my memoirs). Rhodes was godfather to George Paton's first child; Paton married my grandmother's sister when he was fifty-eight and she was eighteen. They had seven children and were married for thirty-three years. The last born were twins, Mary and Peggy, at which stage Grandfather George was in his mid-seventies.

George was well educated with a degree in Geology from Glasgow University. He followed his dreams, first to the goldfields of Ballarat and Bendigo in Australia, then to California and finally to South Africa. He prospected for diamonds in the Kimberley/Barkly West/Harts River area but ironically it was cattle and sheep farming that brought him wealth. In the 1880s and 1890s he owned numerous farms and ran 10,000 head of cattle and 100,000 sheep.

The Boer War cost him dearly, as did the cattle disease rinderpest. Early in the Boer War (late 1890s) the Boers were fighting a guerrilla war. They were wonderful marksmen who shot game from childhood as part of their livelihood. They were highly mobile in small mounted groups who ambushed the British in their bright red uniforms then disappeared into nowhere, only to regroup some days later and stage another ambush. They travelled by night, living off the land plus a bit of maize and biltong (salted dried game meat) carried in their saddle bags, sometimes returning to their farms to regroup and see their families.

The British were not accustomed to being the underdog in a military conflict so General Roberts decided something had to be done and he launched a scorched earth campaign against the Boers. The British were mobilised and worked their way systematically from south to north pillaging every Boer farm on their way. The women and children were put into concentration camps. No stock was left on the Boer farms.

George Paton, being a loyal British citizen, was spared by the British and kept his large flocks of sheep and herds of cattle, but not for long. The Boers figured he was fair game and livestock was systematically pillaged. In the 1940s my brother and I spent many a great holiday on the Paton farm, called "Newlands", where there was good springbok and guineafowl shooting and we were allowed to hunt on the farm. Four of the Paton sisters never married. They lived all their lives somewhat isolated on the family farm. My mother blamed their mother who was jealous of any suitor who sought the affections of one of her daughters. The suitor was never good enough in her view. They were such nice women who would have made good wives and good mothers.

No more diversions, I will now stick to the main subject of this story — which is Mafeking and the family. True assessment would have to accept that Mafeking was not a pretty town, nor is the surrounding countryside, but its history since white settlement has a worthwhile story to tell. The countryside around Mafeking is dead flat — not a hill to be seen. Cecil Rhodes' railway had by the 1890s been constructed to reach Zimbabwe (in those days called Rhodesia after Rhodes) and beyond. A railway line was about this time completed from Johannesburg to join the line to Rhodesia at Mafeking so the town became an important railway junction with big railway workshops. For a few brief years I attended school at the Roman Catholic convent in Mafeking which was on the opposite side of the town to where we lived. Those who worked in the railway workshops were mainly Afrikaans and there was still strong anti-British sentiment because of the injustice the British had inflicted on their women in the concentration camps during the Boer War. As previously mentioned, when I rode to school on my bicycle I had to pass through the housing area that accommodated the railway workers and they often threw stones at me. I was never actually hit but I was terrified. I was about ten or eleven years old. The next year I was sent to boarding school in Cape Town so my bicycle rides through hostile territory ceased.

In the 1880s, certain tribal chiefs sought the protection of the British to prevent what they believed was a desire of the Boers to take over their land, as had happened in the country to the south. Without going into detail as to how this came about, Britain took what is now Botswana under its wing as protector. Mafeking was by then an established town so the British decided to establish their administrative headquarters for Botswana in Mafeking, although this meant that the so-called capital of Botswana was now located outside its own borders. The British had control of the land on both sides of the border so this unusual arrangement caused no problems.

This anomaly was partly overcome by excising about twenty square kilometres of country a few kilometres from Mafeking and naming it the "Imperial Reserve". The offices and some of the residential houses were built on this land which was close enough to link into the Mafeking electricity, water and other services. The capital of the country located outside its own borders persisted until the 1960s when a new capital of Botswana was established at Gaborone in Botswana,

150 kilometres north of Mafeking on the railway line.

Dad died in 1950 and my mother continued to live in Mafeking until 1983 when she died. My uncle Spencer Minchin (my mother's brother) and his family maintained the family connection and one of their sons, Don Minchin, worked as a lawyer in the family legal firm Minchin and Kelly until he died tragically from complications of pneumonia in 2013.

St John's Anglican Church in Mafeking and the town cemetery have strong associations with both the Minchins and the Netteltons. In the cemetery the graves of the following family members will be found.

Millicent Minchin (died aged 18 months in 1896 – my mother's sister who she never knew).
Augustus Minchin (died 1936. My grandfather)
Gerald Nettelton (died 1950. My father)
Agnes Minchin (died 1974. My grandmother)
Ina Eales (died 1968. My mother's sister)
Connie Minchin (died 1984. Wife of Spencer Minchin)
Spencer Minchin (died 1987. My mother's brother)
Helen Nettelton (died 1984. My mother – born a Minchin)
William Brown (died 1979. My mother's second husband)
Donald Minchin (died 2013, aged early 50s. Son of Spencer and Connie Minchin)
Pete Minchin (died 2018, aged 62. Son of Spencer and Connie Minchin.

But I haven't finished with Mafeking yet! Mafeking had lost its claim to the capital of Botswana, but a few years later it found itself once again a capital, this time to the newly established South African Bantustan, or homeland, of Bophuthatswana. Let me explain. The way in which the Afrikaner Nationalist Government of South Africa sought to justify its apartheid policy of separation of the races was to establish a series of black mini states which were theoretically given autonomy within their own area of jurisdiction. The land allotted by South Africa for the mini states collectively comprised just thirteen per cent of the land area of South Africa and was located mainly in underdeveloped areas. The Nationalist Government argued that the African population now had their own territory over which they had complete autonomy, just as the whites had in the land designated as theirs. The Africans had consequently not been discriminated against because they had been given their own land just as the whites had their land. The black people working and living on white-designated land were not its citizens and were expected to abide by the laws of the land that hosted them, a position taken by every country in the world.

This policy was designed by Dr Hendrik Verwoerd who was murdered on the floor of the South African Parliament in 1966. But the policy was rigorously enforced by his successors until the almost miraculous and peaceful end to apartheid in 1994 engineered by Nelson Mandela and Dr F.W. (Frederik Willem) De Klerk of the Nationalist Party. One of the outcomes of these huge political changes in South Africa was the abolition of the Bantustan mini states, of which Bophuthatswana was one, and their absorption back into South Africa. This saw the end of apartheid and every African would have welcomed this but for Mafeking. It meant the end of buckets of money pumped into Bophuthatswana and thus Mafeking by the South African government which had sought to establish good relations with all African-governed regimes, such as the Bantustans Lesotho and Botswana, and this co-operation was worth millions of extra dollars.

Spencer and Connie Minchin (my aunt and uncle) worked closely and productively with the Bophuthatswana President and Connie became principal of the High School which established a very good reputation for good behaviour and academic achievement. Connie was awarded the Order of the Leopard by the President and the Connie Minchin School in Mmbatho, Mafeking, was named in her honour. Spencer Minchin, as was his father, was the legal adviser to many of the senior chiefs in Botswana.

During WWII, Spencer flew Dakota transport planes in North Africa and Europe for five full years. (After the end of the war he bought his own single-engine plane and continued to fly for the next thirty-five years. He never insured his planes and never had a mishap.) Neither Spencer nor his father ever went on an overseas holiday — they maintained that Mafeking was where they wanted to be. It is remarkable that my grandfather, Spencer Minchin, a product of English private education, a graduate of one of the most prestigious law centres in Britain and with a multitude of blue-blood relatives in England and Ireland, never once in sixty-five years paid a visit back to England. He certainly had the money to do it. He owned a number of farms near Mafeking and he bought the Madibe gold mine twenty kilometres south of Mafeking. I believe it never made much money for him and he eventually sold it. My uncle Spencer Minchin was a pillar of the Anglican Church in Mafeking and when it was no longer possible to find an ordained Anglican priest, Spencer took the church over and kept the services going every Sunday with himself in the pulpit. The Archbishop of the Diocese made him an honorary bishop.

In the nineteenth century, the Siege of Mafeking and its final relief was a well-known historical event and promoted by the British as a great military triumph during the Boer War. When news reached London that on May 17, 1900, Mafeking had been relieved, there was much rejoicing. Crowds took to the streets in many English cities to celebrate and the word "Maffick" was added to the English vocabulary. Though the word is no longer commonly used, it is still there to this day in the Oxford English Dictionary meaning to "rejoice joyously". (See Volume III for the full story.)

A few family facts about the Siege of Mafeking: My grandfather and grandmother and my then three-year-old mother stayed in Mafeking throughout the Siege. I have written about the Siege in a separate story in this memoir so I won't go into great detail here, but the Siege was another significant event to add to the other events which combine to create a colourful historical past for this seemingly very ordinary little South African town.

There are a few more experiences in the colourful history of Mafeking which are worth a mention.

Sol Plaatje — Siege of Mafeking — African Diarist

Sol Plaatje was a well known and much respected African author and politician. He was born in the Transvaal in 1870 and educated at a mission school. Despite all the disadvantages of being African in a white-dominated South Africa and also not growing up with English as his home language, he wrote extensively in English, dealing with issues of the day — mainly those that affected Africans, but he also translated four of Shakespeare's plays into Tswana (his home language). Despite the nature of his political writings he never fell foul of the law or suffered any personal persecution. Ultimately he became President of the African People's Congress in 1913. He was greatly respected by both black and white people throughout South Africa.

His association with Mafeking came to pass when he was sent there as a government employee and paid interpreter and was working in Mafeking throughout the siege 1899-1900. He wrote a daily diary. Over the years, a total of eighteen Siege diaries have surfaced; Sol Plaatje's diary is the only one written by an African. I have never read it myself but Connie Minchin (my aunt) was an authority on the Siege and she maintained that of the eighteen she'd read, Plaatje's was the best.

He retained his association with Mafeking throughout his life. Sol Plaatje was undoubtedly a brilliant and deep-thinking man and Mafeking can be proud of its association with him.

AWB Attack on Mafeking

In the 1990s Mafeking became the venue for a totally hare-brained escapade when mem-bers of the ultra-right-wing Afrikaner Resistance Movement (usually known as AWB) under the leadership of Eugene Terre'Blanche randomly attacked Mafeking residents, killing forty-two people.

Three AWB members were shot dead by members of the Bophuthatswana Defence Force. The perception appeared to be that other white people would rise up against the African authorities and join the AWB armed group. They were joined by some of the local white or black population but armed local black police and army soon quelled the uprising. Shortly after the incident and in a climate of widespread revolt, Chief Lucas Mangope was removed from power. All in all it was an unbelievably stupid and counterproductive escapade by the AWB.

A Few Special Memories of Mafeking

Remembered for the wrong reasons

Lorna Clarke was someone I always remember from Mafeking days for the wrong reasons. Her maiden name was Goodyear and her father was considered to be one of the original elite of Mafeking. Their origins were Victorian genteel. Lorna married "Clarkie" Clarke who kept a "weekend" mistress at Lichtenburg — common knowledge to all. Lorna appeared to accept it. Lorna had a general store in Shippard Street, Mafeking. Africans had to ask permission to come into the shop and were treated with disdain. Lorna was a blatant racist. Why they ever shopped in her store I don't know. We all had a giggle when the sanitary bucket cart broke down opposite her shop one night and remained there in all its smelly glory all day. In later years she ran a florist shop. There was an occasion when an African in the employ of the local undertaker was sent to fetch a wreath from her shop. She wouldn't let him into the shop so he had to return without the wreath. He told his employer that when Lorna died he was going to make sure she was put into the freezer alongside the blackest African corpse available. Lorna lived with her two sisters, Dotty and Maude. When Dotty was very ill, their faithful African maid nursed Dotty day and night at home. Lorna allowed her to sleep on a rug under the dining room table! Lorna was a regular churchgoer.

Christmas Greeting

Mrs Webster was sitting on the toilet on Christmas Eve. (In those days there was no water-borne sanitation – the loo was in the back yard with the sanitary bucket collected through a flap which opened from the sanitary lane, which ran along the back fence.) All of a sudden, as she sat there, the lavatory flap was pulled open, the bucket was withdrawn and a beaming black face peered up at Mrs Webster by way of her bare white bottom and shouted "Happy Christmas, Madam".

Grief Gone Wrong

Mr Mogg, the Mafeking mail proprietor, committed suicide in his house using a handgun. Spencer Minchin went to the house to console the grieving widow. He sat with her and after a while she asked to be left alone for a few minutes while she packed a suitcase. Spencer went to wait in an adjoining room. Within minutes she had shot herself dead.

The Pointer and the Partridge

Mr Bernard, the Town Clerk, was a bit of a wag. He was a keen sportsman and liked bird shooting. He had a well trained German Pointer dog which would sniff the birds out in the grass and when it found one it would freeze rigid with nose directed towards the hidden bird and its tail stiff and straight at rear. One day Mr Bernard lost his dog whilst out bird shooting. He called and called but the dog never returned to him and he eventually had to leave without it. A year later he went hunting in the same area. Lo and behold he came across the skeleton of the dog still upright in pointing position and not far from the skeletal nose was the weathered carcass of a partridge! Mr Bernard swore his story was true.

Doorstop Danger

The Leach Family had a 20lb shell used as a doorstop in their house. This was in the early 1950s. It had been lobbed into Mafeking by the Boers during the siege in 1900. How it came to them was unknown but it was presumed to be defused. Their nine-year-old son and two other little boys, when no parents were around. decided they would melt it down for the lead — little boys will be little boys with crazy ideas at times! The shell exploded and killed all three of them.

Dentist's Chevrolet

Dr Bill Brown, the Mafeking Dentist, bought a new Chevrolet car in 1939. In 1960, when he and my mother got married, he bought a new car. The Chevrolet had done 20,000 miles in twenty-one years.

Rail Journey

The rail journey from Mafeking to Cape Town was approximately 1,300kms. Over an eight-year period I travelled on the train for holidays back and forth Mafeking-Cape Town-Mafeking regularly. I estimate I travelled 100,000 kilometres on that train over those eight years. Those were the days of steam engines and compartments upholstered in green leather with hand-tooled woodwork — four persons in first class and six in second class. Definitely whites only. The nonwhites travelled third class in coaches up front just behind the engine where the soot from the engine was worst. The "bedding boy" would come round in the late afternoon and make up the beds — white starched sheets and pillowcases. In a second class compartment the middle bunk was put down to make for six bunks. I always tried to get the top bunk which then became your private domain for the whole trip day or night. The two bottom bunks became day time seats for everyone and the middle bunks were pushed up and secured during the day, so the top bunk was the place to be. I enjoyed the train journeys — reading, eating, talking, sleeping and looking out of the window!

Mafeking Golf Course

My brother and I played regularly on the Mafeking Golf Course during school and university holidays. The greens were oiled gravel and the fairways mowed "veld". We played preferred lie because when you came up to your ball it was quite likely lying in an unplayable depression in the middle of the fairway.

Bobby Locke, five times British Open Champion, came to play in Mafeking. He said the golf course was the hardest he had ever played on! (The ground was so hard.)

The Mafeking Cemetery

Many of our family are buried in the Mafeking Cemetery. The first to be buried there was Millicent Minchin, my mother's elder sister, who died at the age of eighteen months well before my mother was born. As the years went by Millicent was joined in the cemetery by Grandad and Granny Minchin, Ina Eales, my father and others. At the age of eighty my mother was still making the weekly or fortnightly pilgrimage to the cemetery to put flowers on all the family graves — even Millicent's, the sister she never knew who had died eighty-four years before.

The Nelson Girls — A Tragedy

The Nelson girls were blonde and both were really pretty and intelligent. They were aged fifteen and seventeen. One Sunday afternoon, their father allowed a young male friend of theirs to borrow his car to take the two girls out for a drive. He stopped and got out of the car to open a farm gate but did not put on the hand brake or leave it in gear. The car rolled backwards, went over an embankment and landed on its hood. Both girls were killed instantly. The Nelsons had no other children.

A Belting for Pinching some Apple Tart

Mum told my brother and I we were not allowed any more apple tart. We crept into the pantry after lunch and were demolishing the rest of the tart when we were caught red-handed. I was five and Gerald was seven. Dad belted me twice on the backside with his belt — not hard. Gerald talked himself out of it — I felt a sense of great injustice. It was the only time Dad beat me.

Boarding at Rondebosch Boys' High School

Cape Town, 1944–48

In January 1944 I went off to Rondebosch Boys High boarding school in Cape Town. My brother was entering his third year when I arrived so I had the advantage that he could settle me in.

I was a bit unhappy for the first week or two but soon acclimatised myself and, looking back on five years as a boarder at Rondebosch, I can say that I enjoyed it. I was fortunate that I was good at sport and my lessons didn't cause me too much trouble, although I was not particularly clever, so the ingredients were there for easy acceptance by my fellow students and the avenues to indulge myself in sport without those complicating academic problems.

Rondebosch is a school with a very fine reputation built on magnificent grounds in the shadow of the Table Mountain. The Headmaster was Wally Mears who was successful in negotiation with the Government for funding and the boarding house was divided into two separate houses, both of them very high class,

The new boy arrives.

certainly by the standards of those days. I was in Mason House where the set-up consisted of six to a dormitory. My Housemaster was a Mr Fox, always known as Foxy, who was a heavy-smoking bachelor who could be very strict but also very kind. My main friends in those early days were a David Grant, son of a chemist who had a pharmacy in Hermanus, about a hundred and fifty kilometres from Cape Town. There was also Clive Hirschon, a Jewish student, whose parents owned a string of watch and jewellery shops. I don't know why it turned out that way, but Clive and I, from the age of twelve, between breakfast and going to school always went to the common room and read the newspaper. It's a habit that has stayed with me for the rest of my life. I read all the latest news on the Second World War and South African politics and the sport that was going on in South Africa every single day.

Alongside Mason House, which was for the younger boarders, was "Canigou", which was a new boarding house where the boarders had cubicle bedrooms to themselves. Each little bedroom had its own bed and locker and you were allowed to plug in your earphones and listen to the radio every night until ten o'clock. This sort of set-up was pretty well unheard of in those days and we can thank Wally Mears for the strategic and progressive thinking that he put into the development of Rondebosch Boys High.

In Mason House we were allowed to have our own crystal sets with earphones and we were able to listen to the radio in that way. The old crystal set was something unique. I can't explain how it worked but you had a little bit of crystal, which looked like an ordinary piece of rock, and you had an arm with a little wire on it and you moved the wire around on the crystal, and there was an electric current somewhere mixed up into it and it performed as a radio. I'm no electrician or radio mechanic and I really don't know how it all fitted together but suffice to say a very basic-looking crystal set was able to pick up radio waves and transmit them into normal tones in your earphones.

The routine at boarding school was that we got up at 6.30 and had a shower. Fortunately the showers were hot: it was not the "development of character" type of treatment which is so indicative of the English public schools that you had to bring people up tough if they were to be good citizens

and make their way in life. So it was not hard getting out of bed at 6.30 and into the shower. We had study period from 7 o'clock to 7.40 before going to breakfast. The dining room was in "Canigou". You had to be out of breakfast by 8.15 and the school bell rang at 8.45. The school building in those days was on Camp Ground Road which was a walk of about five or six minutes from the boarding school. It was an old-style sandstone building. The design was double-storey classrooms all the way around a central quadrangle. One of the joys of those days was the lunch break, when we walked back to "Canigou" for lunch which was served in the dining room and if one had the money, the ice cream cart was always positioned outside the school. It was a horse-drawn cart with a coloured attendant and the ice creams cost "thruppence".

The main ice cream on sale was vanilla with two wafers. I always enjoyed my ice cream and still do.

In 1944 when I first went to Rondebosch my pocket money allocation was one shilling per week. Ice creams, as I have said, cost thruppence and chocolate bars were the same. So, with the shilling one could afford two ice creams and two chocolate bars for the week and that was it. Some of us had a bit of spare pocket money sent to us by parents or relations for a birthday and this helped a lot. Auntie Madge was always very good to me; she never forgot my birthday and always sent £5 which really was much appreciated.

School came out at 3pm and we then had three hours for sport before going in to supper at 6pm. The two boarding houses were located on the edge of the very extensive grounds of Rondebosch so we were well positioned to make the most of the sporting opportunities. The grounds consisted of seven sports fields with an avenue of oaks going down and dividing the sporting grounds, then the Black River which was tree-lined cut diagonally across the property. It really was extremely beautiful because the oak trees must have been hundreds of years old and were very high and leafy and were inhabited by numerous red squirrels which lived on the acorns. Along the Black River we used to build wooden tree houses right up in amongst the branches. Some of

High School on Camp Ground Road.

The Black River flowed through Rondebosch sports grounds. We had seven ovals.

them were really quite substantial. No-one ever asked questions as to where the timber came from and they must have known that it could only have been filched from surrounding building sites. I can recall going out once, and it was only once, and I was terrified to filch some building timber. It meant climbing out of the boarding school window during the night and going to the building site and, accompanied by a friend, carrying the timber back to the school grounds. I guess it was a peer group thing because you were nobody if you didn't have your tree house. I can recall that I really didn't want to go out and steal that wood but then if I didn't we wouldn't have a tree house and you went down a notch on the social scale. The tree houses were used quite a lot by the smokers. We never used ours that way because none of my group ever smoked.

When I arrived at Rondebosch I had never participated at any sort of school competitive sport and I had never realised that I was quite good at sport. In my first year I found myself doing well in athletics. I ran in the Under 12 group and came second in both the one hundred and two hundred yards — I was beaten by my rival, Lionel Duffy. The two of us were then selected to run in the Triangular Athletics Competition which was held annually between Rondebosch, Bishops (Diocesan College) and the South African College School. To my surprise in the Triangular Competition Lionel Duffy came first in both the one hundred and two hundred yards and I came second in both. It is a strong recollection that after performing well in athletics my status amongst my fellow students rose and I was very conscious of it.

In the second term the rugby season opened and I found myself playing on the wing for the Under 12As. It is quite remarkable that in those days Rondebosch High School had fifteen rugby teams in the various age categories competing in competitions with other schools in a league, which meant matches were held every Saturday morning throughout the second and third terms. In each league there would have been about twelve schools from around the Cape Peninsula competing.

To clarify, the Under 13A, Under 13B, Under 13C and Under 13D played a match against another school every single Saturday and the same went for the Under 15s, Under 16s and Under 19s. Rugby was a religion with us. Being boarders living right on the playing fields, we were allowed to take out a rugby ball after school and we frequently did this and kicked around and organised our own little matches, so we were always participating and we were very fit indeed.

We had organised practice once a week and every single team had a School Master coaching and organising them. It did not matter whether you were in an A team or an E team, you had a Master who took your practice and would accompany you to your match on a Saturday because sometimes they would be at fairly far-flung school grounds around the Cape Peninsula. This system produced a lot of good rugby players and the school has a fine record in producing inter-provincial and international players.

At boarding school the food is always an important factor and I'm happy to say that the food at Rondebosch was good. We had porridge every morning for breakfast and eggs six days a week and on Fridays, no doubt in deference to those who were Catholic, we had fish, usually smoked cod which is quite pleasant when cooked properly. Our lunch and evening meals were quite substantial and we ate a lot of meat and good vegetables. In looking back, it's an interesting reflection how little we were affected by the War which was at that time raging in Africa and Europe and the Pacific area. There was never any food shortage and there was no fighting on South African soil. Of course, one was aware of all those men who fought in the South African army, navy or air force and occasionally there would be those who one learnt had been killed. I think one of the few things that we had to suffer was that our bread for about three years was not wheaten but was made of rye.

All the wheaten products went up north to feed the troops.

In the dining room we sat at tables of twelve with a Prefect at the head of each table and a group of boarding house School Masters sat at the top table and kept an eye on things.

Rondebosch was a four-term school which meant that we had six weeks' holiday over Christmas, one week at Easter, four weeks in June/July and one week at Michaelmas. One of the problems this created for my brother and myself was that it was not always easy for us to get home for the short holidays because they were so short and the journey from Cape Town to Mafeking, where my parents were living, took two nights and a day. Also in those days Dad, with three children at boarding school and on a British Colonial Service salary, did not have much money to throw around. We frequently did get home for those short holidays but there were occasions when we couldn't and we would go to stay with families of friends.

I always enjoyed the train journeys because in those days South African railways were very comfortable. We always travelled second class which meant that we were in compartments of six. There was the bottom bunk and the top bunk which were non-moving fixtures then there was a middle bunk which you put up at night on either side of the compartment. Each compartment, even in second class, had its own wash basin with hot and cold water and there was a table which could be let down in the centre of the compartment and you sat on the bunks on either side and could use it for eating or playing cards or whatever. The compartments were wood-panelled with original leather seating — there were no plastic products in those days. The train always had a dining car and you could go in and get a good meal for about five shillings. Every morning at 6.30 the steward would come round and bang on the door of your compartment and offer you a cup of tea or coffee which you could drink in bed. If you wanted a proper breakfast you had to go into the dining car. In the evenings the bedding boy would come around with the railway linen and blankets and would lay your bed for you. The linen was always beautifully starched and the bed cost five shillings. You kept your bed in your compartment for the duration of your journey. There was a toilet at either end of the carriage but there were no showers. I used to spend a lot of time looking out of the window. You could pull the window down and lean out and you always had to be careful that you didn't look up towards the engine with your eyes open because you were liable to get an eyeful of soot. In those days the engines were all steam driven and if you left the window of your compartment open for too long you would quite possibly gather a lot of soot in the compartment. The trains generally ran very much to time and were pleasant to travel on, particularly if you were travelling with a group of fellow school mates which was often the case. Rondebosch had a number of boarders from Southern Rhodesia and Northern Rhodesia. Those who came from Northern Rhodesia spent three nights and two days on the train to get home.

At school over the weekends we would normally play sport on a Saturday morning, either cricket or rugby depending on the season, and then would be required to be back at school for lunch. After lunch in the rugby season we were allowed to go to Newlands Rugby Ground to watch the senior club sides play and we went religiously every Saturday and took a very keen interest in the senior teams. Newlands is a rugby ground which has many memories for me because in my older days I played rugby there quite frequently. My school mates and myself knew all the players in the senior teams and in the international arena and we talked expansively on team selections and the performance of individuals and so on. Being the War years, there was no international rugby being played in South Africa but the Provincial teams still met and these were exciting matches.

On Saturday evenings we still had to do one hour study and we were allowed a bit of time to just relax and do nothing but the study periods were fairly consistent throughout the week, and as I've said, even on a Saturday evening. On a normal weekday we had forty minutes study in the morning before school from 7 to 7.40am and then in the evenings from 7 to 8.30 or 9.30pm depending on the age group you were in. The study was always supervised by a Master so there certainly was plenty of time to do your homework (and we got plenty of it) and to do your reading. On Sunday evenings we had a religious service which was non-denominational from 7 to 8.30pm and each Sunday we were expected to write a letter home and most of us did. I wrote home every weekend for five years and Mum kept all my letters. To my great disappointment when Mum died and I was in Australia, Connie Minchin took control of Mum's flat and threw out all my letters. She never even asked me.

Rondebosch was a school which attracted quite a few Afrikaans-speaking families mainly from the old Cape Huguenot stock. Many of them came from very old wine-making families or farmers of some sort. Names such as Starke, Melck, du Plessis and de Villiers were the sort of names which, when you look at the history of the school, occur generation after generation and I have no doubt that's still the case. So I heard a lot of Afrikaans spoken and by the time I left Rondebosch at the end of 1948 I understood Afrikaans perfectly and could speak it, but for some reason never really spoke it as much as I should have done. I got a very good mark for Afrikaans in Matric then never used it again because at Cape Town University I didn't hear much Afrikaans spoken and then when I went to Basutoland it was never used, so my knowledge of it dissipated over the years, which was in some ways a pity.

I wrote my Junior Certificate in 1946 and got a First Class but when I did Matric I didn't get that First Class which I had hoped for and had to settle for a Second Class, but when I think back on it now, it really wasn't important in my life.

Rondebosch was a big school and my year, right from Standard 6 up to Matric, consisted of between ninety and one hundred and ten students in ech year. We were generally divided into four classes, sometimes five, and each year had a set of teachers. For instance, the Maths teacher for that particular year would rotate between the four or five classes and the same with the English teacher etc. I was never quite sure whether it was to my credit or not but although I didn't excel academically I could claim a tremendous consistency in my class placing. In five years' high school I never came higher than twelfth or lower than twenty-first in the average of one hundred students in the year. Geography was always my best subject and I excelled at it. My worst subject

Now a senior student in long pants.

was Latin which I took in my first year at school, failed dismally and I was allowed by my parents to drop it in Standard 7.

In many ways the modern student has it a lot easier academically than we did. Think back about calculations. There were no calculators, you depended on your knowledge of your ten times tables. We had to deal with twelve pence to a shilling and twenty shillings to the pound, and twelve inches to the foot, three feet to the yard and 1,760 yards to the mile, and 4,480 square feet to the acre. When you had to do multiplications and additions it was very complex indeed. Adding up columns of figures with no calculators required a lot of concentration and then you had to add it all up again to double check. It took an awful long time. These days with our decimal system and computers and calculators and all our electronic equipment, it makes life very easy compared to what we had to endure as students of mathematics — and even in your everyday life.

Then there was of course no TV. As I've mentioned, we had our earphones that we could use in the evenings when we went to bed to listen to the radio. Radio was nowhere near as sophisticated in those days as it is now. SABC (South African Broadcasting Corporation) only operated for a certain number of hours per day. There was an English program and an Afrikaans program and nothing more. There were no commercial programs, there were no different South African broadcasting corporations or wavelengths to pick up. The first South African commercial channel, Springbok Radio, came into operation in the early 1950s. It is quite funny to reflect that one of the popular radio stations in the early 1950s was Mafeking Radio. This radio station operated for two hours in the evening and because there was nothing else to listen to, was very popular throughout South Africa. It was simply a case of playing music and they had provision for people to write in with requests. Wally Coombs, chubby with horn-rimmed glasses, became quite a celebrity! The radio room for Mafeking Radio was on the Imperial Reserve and was originally established to provide easy and quick communication between the Government headquarters for Bechuanaland Protectorate and the various offices within Bechuanaland itself. Someone gave permission for this radio station to operate a two-hour program in the evenings and it became a real success until some ten years later when it was completely swamped by the establishment of numerous new commercial radio stations in South Africa.

When I was at school we were allowed out two weekends a term, and our sporting schedules were organised in such a way that on those particular weekends we didn't have to participate in sport. We were allowed to go out with friends or relatives or if we had no-one available we could get special permission to go to the Bioscope in Cape Town.

It was a great thing to go to a Bio Cafe which consisted of a cinema which ran for the whole day and well into the night and whilst you were watching the film you were served a milkshake or a cup of tea or whatever your choice was. When the film ended you did not necessarily have to leave the cinema, you could simply change your seat and stay on if you wished. It cost one shilling and sixpence to go to the Bio Cafe. There were three of them in Cape Town, all fairly seedy affairs but we used to love them because we got a milkshake. There were other cinemas where we paid a shilling entrance fee. The Alhambra was an opulent, art deco type cinema which rather tragically was knocked down in the 1970s when the new Cape Town foreshore development took place.

Back to boarding school. As a young teenager I had rotten teeth. By the age of thirteen I had fillings in just about every tooth in my head including my front teeth. The dentist had his surgery in a building just opposite the Rondebosch Station and how I hated that building. In those days there were no injections and the drill was a clumsy, grinding affair which, as it warmed up and got

A weekend out. Mum and Dad were staying at Fish Hoek hotel and I was allowed out from boarding school. Clockwise from back left: Elizabeth Meyer, Felicité Nairn, Marygold Brooks, Spencer (Ted). (See Meyer, Ellenberger, Pagewood family stories in Volume III.)

towards the nerve, hurt like hell. When I was a bit younger I had to have some teeth pulled out and went to Dr Brown, the dentist in Mafeking, who many years later became my stepfather, and he used a gas mask on me. I was about six and I have vivid recollections of this gas mask being put over my nose; I went berserk and pulled the mask out of his hand and dashed out the door, only to be recaptured by my mother outside the house and brought back. The dentist's chair was an awful place in those days. My mother was extremely conscientious about our teeth and she insisted that I went to the dentist every six months and it was a good thing because I probably would have false teeth by now if that had not been the case. As it turned out my teeth were continually filled until I was in my early twenties then all of a sudden I found myself with hardly ever having a filling and now, sixty years later, I still have my teeth. I still go to the dentist regularly for checkups and it is a far less painful exercise nowadays than it was then.

I did not have too many bad experiences with the Masters at school. On one occasion Civvi Olivier, who was my Maths teacher, brought me up to the blackboard in front of the class to do some mathematical calculation and I got it wrong and he kneed me up the backside pretty hard, in fact I really felt quite ill for twenty-four hours or so, but I got over it. There was a Mr Minnaar who in latter years also taught me Maths and he used to wander up and down between the desks to check on how you were going and if you were getting something wrong he got a key and used the sharp edge on the lobe of your ear, using the thumb to really make it hurt. There was "Cross Eye" Hullic who had a squint and taught me English. I was sitting in the front desk and he always used to rub the front of his pants against the front desk and so we used to spread chalk along the front edge so that his pants by the end of a period were covered in white dust. He used to get really

A night spent in the Mountain Club hut on top of Table Mountain.

mad and there was an occasion when he got my friend Clive Hirschaun by the hair and accused him of being the perpetrator and I said, "Sir, you always pick on the small boys." He went mad and just about annihilated me.

Steyn Krige never taught me but for two years he was my rugby coach and I got on extremely well with him. He was very strict and when boys did not have friends or relatives to go to over weekends when we were allowed out he would take us climbing Table Mountain and we would spend two nights in the mountain huts up on the slopes of the mountain. I went with him on a number of occasions and thoroughly enjoyed it. Another Master I remember well was Stan Atkins, a very Christian person, but nice and he taught geography. Wally Mears was our Headmaster and an outstanding personality. You couldn't help but remember him. I corresponded with him for a number of years after I left school until he died. He later became Headmaster of the new St Stithians College in Johannesburg which he planned in many ways based on the concepts of Rondebosch. St Stithians school was partly attributable to the efforts of Gail's grandfather, Charles Leake*, who was a leading Johannesburg financier, and donated part of the land upon which the school is built. The foundation stone of St Stithians was laid by Charles Leake. St Stithians is now a very well known school in South Africa. One of the four houses that make up St Stithians is called Leake House.

Prefects used "lines" as punishment. The following lines in large script one hundred times takes up considerable time which could have been spent at leisure. "I must not be overcome by the exuberance of my own verbosity."

I didn't often get into trouble at school. On only two occasions I did get the cane. On the

---

* For more detail on Charles Leake, see Volume V

other hand Gerald, my brother, got caned quite a few times. He was caught smoking on a number of occasions which was always worth six of the best.

Boarding school was quite a good experience for me. I enjoyed the sport, I had no great problems with my lessons, I had a lot of friends and there was always companionship. It taught me self confidence and independence early in my life. It must have been hard on my parents, I would personally not enjoy having my children go away to boarding school from the age of nine onwards and only see them during the holidays. However, I guess in those days parents accepted that that was what would happen. Particularly Colonial Service parents who lived in remote areas. Even in Lesotho where schools were not that far away, many of the children of my colleagues were sent to school in England and sometimes saw their parents only once a year.

My one regret at school was that I matriculated at the age of sixteen and was never able to play sport for the senior team. My rugby at Rondebosch in my final year was for the Under 16A team. We had a good team and we only lost one match and that was to our arch-rivals, Bishops. We beat them once and they beat us once and in the league we finished on equal points. When I went on to university I found myself playing in the same university team as a lot of my Bishops' rivals. In the athletics arena I continued to do well right up to the time I left school. In the 4 x 110 yards relay I shared the school record with the other three who made up the relay team and that record stood for fourteen years.

After leaving school I did not keep up with most of my high school friends. I tended to form new friendships at university and not a lot of my school friends found their way to Cape Town University. They seemed to spread themselves all over the place and only a few came on to Cape Town with me.

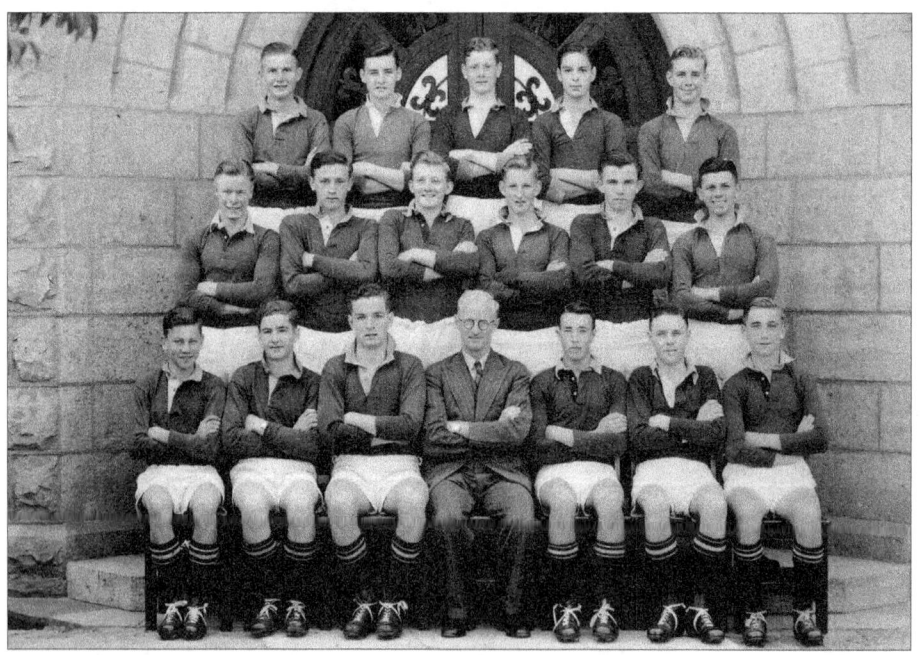

Under 16A team which shared equal top spot in the league with Bishops. I am front row, second from left.

Cape Town University is located on the slopes of Table Mountain, Devils Peak — a superb setting.

Cape Town University
1949-52

I matriculated in December 1948 and had a glorious three-month holiday before going on to Cape Town University, where I enrolled for a Bachelor of Arts in Native Administration.

I was lucky to obtain accommodation in Smuts Hall, a residence on the campus. In Smuts Hall there were about three hundred students, all male, while on the other side of the campus was Fuller Hall, which was of identical design with three hundred female students in residence. It was a great-set up, to be right on campus within five minutes walking distance of the lecture theatres and to have a women's residence with three hundred girls in it a stone's throw away. Right below our residence were two sports fields which we used regularly as an outlet for our rugby enthusiasm.

During the rugby season I had an organised practice on a Tuesday, an informal practice on a Wednesday, another formal practice on a Thursday, a match on a Saturday and every so often we had pick-up matches on a Sunday. In other words, I was playing rugby in some form five days a week — and boy was I fit.

Initiation

As a first-year student in Smuts Hall I had to go through an initiation conducted by senior students. We were subjected to all sorts of initiation rituals which had been going on since time immemorial. There were silly things like not being allowed to take out a girl for the first two terms, being required to have all three buttons of our jacket done up at all times, being required to participate in the building of the seniors' floats for the University Rag towards the end of the first term, duties associated with the annual Intervarsity rugby match between Cape Town University and Stellenbosch University, running various errands for seniors and periodically making coffee for them in the evenings subject to a roster. There were regular parades conducted by seniors where we were harangued and told what lumps of turd we were, and tested as to whether we had learnt the university songs in preparation for various occasions such as Intervarsity.

Looking back on it, I feel it did me no harm. It certainly built up a tremendous camaraderie between us first years and made us enter into and understand the traditions of the university. No-one ever suffered any physical harm, just on occasions a bit of a dent in one's pride.

Smuts Hall

Smuts Hall was a well-designed building. It had two quadrangles and, rather on the old English university concept, there were a series of doors around the quadrangle which opened into staircases, each with ten rooms on three floors. Each student had his own room, often with a glorious view out over the Cape Flats towards the Hottentots Holland Mountains and False Bay. We had coffee-making facilities on our staircase and in the first year you were allocated to a staircase strictly on the basis of alphabetical order. In your second year you were allowed to get your own group of ten together and have a staircase formed consisting of your own friends. This we did in our second and third years and it was great fun. There are so many of those people on that staircase I have kept in touch with and continue to keep in touch with, although they are starting to drop off now.

The dining room was situated between the first and second quadrangles. The food was very good and they did well in the manner in which they fed us. In your second year you could choose your table mates and you sat at particular seats. You had to be in meals by a certain time otherwise you just went without your grub.

University Rag

The University Rag was a great occasion. On Rag day the student floats took over the centre of Cape Town and from early in the morning we students spread ourselves right throughout the Cape Peninsula selling the Rag magazine. The idea behind it was to collect money for various charities. On the whole we were tolerated and in many cases were accepted by the Cape Town community who had to put up with a lot of nonsense and hi-jinks from a bunch of over-lively and in some cases inebriated students.

The organisation of the Rag was under the control of a high-powered committee. Looking back on it, many of those students involved in the organisation of the Rag later became leaders in the South African community simply because they had skills and drive and they used the Rag

Left: Smuts Hall, the men's residence where I lodged for three years, is the building on the right.

Below: Initiation made me understand better the traditions of the university. I believe I benefited from the form of initiation I went through. Note the Teddy Bear — the start of my nick name TED which has stayed with me ever since.

We built our own float. The Cape Town University Rag was a big event in the city and closed down traffic for a couple of hours. The crowds were huge.

festival to get themselves some experience. In terms of Adelaide, you could say that the University Rag procession was in similar vein to the John Martin's Christmas Pageant. There would be about thirty to forty floats in the Rag procession — some of them were very clever indeed.

A great deal of work for weeks beforehand went into the design of the floats and the first-year students were very much involved in doing the hard work. Architectural and fine art students participated in making the floats as good as they were. The vehicles for the floats were lent by commercial concerns throughout the Cape Peninsula. They were generous in the manner in which they did this and usually provided a driver on the day as well — just as well, because a lot of those students were not sober throughout that day!

I can remember as a first-year student on Rag day getting up about five o'clock in the morning, because we had been allocated an area to sell the Rag magazine on the other side of the Peninsula, and we had to get there by bus. We were knocking on doors by 7.30 in the morning and then had to be back in town by about 9.30 to join our float. After the float procession it was tradition that all the students flocked down to the Alhambra on the Cape Town foreshore. There would be much hilarity and drinking and singing, and a complete student takeover. As a student it was tremendous fun and the camaraderie was great but I well imagine that the general public used to breathe a sigh of relief when Rag day was over and done with, although I think on the whole they enjoyed the float parade.

Coming at the rear of the procession there was always the Rag Queen, and universities certainly produce some very beautiful girls. In those days there was a long selection process and the attitude towards beauty competitions was different. Most of the girls used to participate. It was considered quite an honour to be selected as the Rag Queen of Cape Town University. All this has, I believe, now disappeared into the annals of history which I regard as being rather sad but times change and I can understand that the modern Cape Town University with its totally different student makeup and attitudes would not have the ingredients for a successful University Rag.

Three Rhodes Scholars

In my second year at university we had a group of ten of us on our staircase which we retained in our third year. Of our group, I can claim that we all did well in our future careers. Three won Rhodes Scholarships and I later met up with them in England when I was at Cambridge.

John Didcott did not win a Rhodes Scholarship but became one of South Africa's most eminent Judges. Vince Rabie became a doctor and practised in Port Elizabeth.

Of the Rhodes Scholars, Dennis Robinson became a Professor of Law at Harare University. He was a Double Oxford Rugby Blue and also played rugby for England. He was a regular member of the Western Province Provincial Team. Ian Reeler did PPE at Oxford although he was an architectural student at Cape Town University and subsequently followed a career in architecture in Sydney. He was also a Double Oxford Rugby Blue and ran as an international athlete in the four hundred metres at the 1948 Olympic Games. I can remember in the year that I was at Cambridge, Ian was big news because he scored an extremely good try in the Oxford-Cambridge University match. Mark Rule was not athletic but was very much a double A student and he subsequently became an executive in one of the big publishing firms in the UK.

Those of us who did not aspire to these high scholarship levels seemed to do well. Mick Roberts became a prominent civil engineer in South Africa, well known in the irrigation and sewerage areas. Mike Clinton had a successful architectural business in Harare. John Naude became a lawyer and worked for one of the big wineries in Cape Town. I followed a career in the British Colonial Service and other things after that and did reasonably well.

Of course one socialised not only with one's fellow students who happened to be on the same staircase and we all had many friends spread across the university, both male and female! Some tended to team up very early on at university with girlfriends and quite a few of them subsequently married and lived happily ever after. Mick Roberts was one of those — he met Pixie when he was in second year at university and they are still together, now retired. They had four children and many grandchildren and I see them when I go back to South Africa.

Rugby: Scoring a Try at Newlands Before a Crowd of 40,000

One of my memories was when we played Stellenbosch University at the famous Newlands Rugby Ground before a crowd of 40,000. It was a curtainraiser to the Interprovincial Western Province versus Transvaal match and I scored a try running half the length of the field down the wing. As a team we had a great year and won the competition. On that occasion when I scored the try we had a really good win over Stellenbosch University, always the biggest challenge of the season.

Looking at the photograph of the Combined University Under 19 Team it is interesting to

Cape Town Stellenbosch Combined U19 Rugby team, 1951. We played the rest of Western Province U19 and won 9-3. I am in the second row, on the right. Of those in the picture, ten went on to play at provincial or national level. I was not one of them.

We socialised a lot. I am in the centre with John Brink and Bruce MacDonald.

reflect on the rugby careers of those in the photograph. Six subsequently played international rugby for South Africa and another four played interprovincial rugby. I was really one of the non-achievers in that I played off and on for Cape Town University First Team but never got anywhere near interprovincial standard.

Golf, Socialising and my First Car

Ian Reeler and I played golf frequently. He had a motor scooter and we used to go off to the golf course on his scooter with two bags of clubs. How on earth that scooter got us back up to the university, which was right up on the slopes of Table Mountain, I do not know. I went out a lot with John Didcott in a social sense. I used to periodically go to Durban and spend a week or so with John staying at his home. He was always a great talker and one always knew that he was going to end up at the Bar and would become a judge; of course one didn't realise how distinguished a judge he would be. John was my best man when Gail and I married.

John was a member of the select group which drew up the new South African Constitution at the end of apartheid. As a judge in South Africa, he was empowered to impose the death penalty. Many did. John refused to ever condemn someone to death in his ten years on the bench.

At university we had a great social time. There were always functions on such as the Engineers' Ball or the Medical Faculty Ball or the Smuts Hall Bi-annual Ball or a party after the rugby match or a weekend at some place near the beach. You always had a group of friends around you and there were always boys and girls and the facility to have a great time. In those days the crime level in Cape Town — and for that matter in South Africa — was extremely low and there were none of the hazards of the present South Africa with its incredible violence and crime. Transport was always a bit of a problem but a smattering of students in first year had cars and by our final year most of us owned some sort of a ramshackle vehicle or clubbed in together to get something.

In my last year John Naude and I bought a 1936 black Hillman for £50 which stood us in really good stead for our time at university. After eighteen monhts we sold it for the same amount that we had bought it for and a couple of weeks later it just disintegrated and the poor person who bought it had to abandon it. Sometimes one is lucky!

No Breathalysers – How did we Survive?

I think all of us would think back in horror at the way we drove in those days. There was nothing like a breathalyser and I am sure we frequently drove well above the 0.05 limit. There were fatalities amongst students but then there are likewise in today's university spheres. I guess one of the factors then was that there was so much less traffic on the roads and vehicles on the whole didn't travel as fast as they do now. There was no driver education and no seat belts. Mick Roberts had a nasty accident with a full car — he was the driver and trying to conduct the chorus and drive round corners at the same time.

I Get my Driver's Licence

I got my driver's licence in Mafeking at the age of seventeen — in fact on my seventeenth birthday. I went to see the Town Clerk who was a family friend and he said, "You've been driving for quite a while haven't you?" To which I replied in the affirmative. I hadn't been driving openly on public roads but he knew that Dad had allowed us to drive when we were in areas where there was no other traffic and on the aerodrome and so on. He got into the car with me, being Dad's car which he had lent me, and I drove round the block with him and he said he considered that I was perfectly competent to drive and issued me with my licence on the spot. My brother and my sister were treated in just the same way.

Left: Kirstenbosch Gardens, Cape Town

Right: Boer War memorial in Cape Town with Table Mountain in the background.

It is Not Wise to go to University Too Young
My children each had a maturing year before university

When I started my first year at Cape Town University we had quite a good number of ex-servicemen studying for their degrees. The maturity of these students compared to a first-year Arts student of seventeen years of age must have been very marked indeed. Looking back I realise that I went to university too young and, although I passed all of my exams in my first year, I really did not appreciate that the university had more to offer in its extra-curricular activities than simply to have a good time socially. I had a wonderful time socially, went to many dances and parties, thoroughly enjoyed my sport, enjoyed the companionship of all my newly found friends in Smuts Hall, had many a convivial get-together at pubs after rugby and so on. It was not until my last year that I started to appreciate what a university had to offer and I was very fortunate to have a second shot at university four years later when I went to Cambridge.

With my own children, Gail and I decided that each child must have a maturing year before going on to university because they completed their Matriculation at an early age. This maturing year worked very well for all three of them. We insisted that year must be devoted to something constructive. Gail took Beverley across to London and launched her into a dress-making and design course. She found Bevie a very nice place to stay at Ames House in Hampstead, a Victorian mansion converted at the turn of the century to "protecting the morals of young working girls". There were seventeen girls in all and they had partial supervision and we always knew that if anything drastic happened we would be advised very soon. Bevie seems to have thoroughly enjoyed that year and she certainly learnt a great deal on her six-month dress-making and design course because when she came home she made all her own clothes and continues to be a real expert in that line. After her six-month course she did some travelling, worked in a variety of casual jobs, and went home via South Africa to see the relatives. The following year she went on to university a far more mature young lady, majored in English and did well.

Tracy in her maturing year spent eight months working for Sid and Sheila Youthed in Botswana. Sid owned a safari company which did three-week safaris into the Western Desert and then up into the Okavango. Tracy was lucky enough to get marooned up a tree by a herd of elephants — her luck was in the form of the other person marooned being a professional photographer from America. They had to stay up the tree for about four hours and during that time Tracy learnt a huge amount about photography. We had bought her a reasonable camera before she left and by the time she came home she was really taking good photographs. Now she is a professional photographer.

Penny did her maturing year in Iceland where she was housekeeper for Pat and Mark Chapman, the British Ambassador. She learnt a lot about running a busy household at a level in which all the social etiquette of the diplomatic world had to be observed. She had a great time mainly because there was a NATO airbase not far from Reykjavik and she and her great mate Edwina got to know quite a number of the pilots and other servicemen associated with the base and they had a great social time. The British admiral who was in charge of the warships in the British segment of the combined USA-UK contingent which made up the NATO force often socialised with the US Air commander and Pat and Mark Chapman (British Ambassador) on occasion joined them. Penny and Edwina also went along and that was how they got to know the American pilots. Penny fell in love with an American Phantom Jet pilot who was at least twelve years her senior. She was seventeen at that stage. In group situations they saw a lot of one another but I don't think he ever took her seriously. Penny came home and successfully completed a Bachelor of Business degree. Ironically Penny married a pilot ten years later. He was Norwegian, not American. As soon as she had completed her degree she set off for Botswana and spent the next three years managing safari lodges in remote areas, always surrounded by prolific wildlife – antelope and those that eat you! Later she worked in a number of countries in various jobs where she performed well at senior level. Then her two boys took over her life – not uncommon amongst mums!

Holidays in Mafeking

During my university days we went home for the long holidays in July and at Christmas time and in little Mafeking there were about fifteen of us students who attended a variety of universities. During the holidays, particularly the long Christmas holiday which for university students amounted to between two and three months, we had frequent social gatherings, usually at one another's homes, and there was the occasional dance in the Town Hall.

My brother and I and Derek Rielly and Alistair Webster were keen on our golf and played endless golf matches on the very hard Mafeking course. In those days there were no grass greens, just oiled gravel. The fairways were cut but were not watered or planted up in any way. We played preferential lie which helped a lot because you never knew whether your ball was going to land up in a dip or not.

How NOT to Handle Alcohol

During my very first university holiday I rather disgraced myself. We went to a dance in the Town Hall and a number of us, halfway through the evening, decided we needed another drink so we went across to the Crewes Hotel and I had three quick brandy and limes. I'm not sure that I had ever drunk brandy and lime in my life before but the effect of those three drinks was pretty devastating and not long after returning to the Town Hall I found myself outside being sick in the gutter. The Reverend Mark Nye saw me and in the next monthly Church newspaper he wrote an editorial about the bad behaviour of the children of the good families of Mafeking. Dad would have read that article and I'm sure he knew something was going on but he never took the matter up with me. Gerald and Elizabeth would never have told our parents what had happened. In any event, on that same evening Gerald got himself into difficulties because he took a lady friend up to the racecourse and got stuck in the mud and in his efforts to get out he wrecked the gearlink of Dad's car. Dad wasn't pleased; I'm not sure what story Gerald told him but I had one over him in that regard so it was just wise for neither of us to say anything. My mother intimated to me years later that Dad was always terrified that this particular young lady, who was a fairly fast mover, was going to allow herself to be trapped by Gerald. Gerald was pretty wild in those days.

As an illustration of this, Gerald, who was in College House, had a best friend called Sharkey King. Sharkey was notorious for his drinking and purposely failed every year so that he didn't have to leave university. He had a posh car and lots of money. Sharkey reformed afterwards and married one of my close university friends, Estelle Phillips. Today Sharkey is regarded as one of the most eminent constitutional lawyers in South Africa. If Gerald was still alive I think he would be quite astonished.

I frequently related to my own children my experience arising from those three short, sharp, brandy and limes. My message to them was that you are allowed to make one mistake but if you don't learn from that mistake and you repeat it, you are being stupid. I can honestly say that I have never again allowed myself to be in a position where alcohol consumption caused me embarrassment. I thoroughly enjoy my alcohol but I am so grateful that I learnt that lesson early in life and that the lesson served me well.

During the Christmas holidays Dad used to find us work in the government. I enjoyed this, particularly because it gave me a bit of extra pocket money. We probably got about six weeks' work with pay and we found ourselves well accepted in the offices in which we worked. I guess this was understandable considering Dad's position in the Service. Dad could be quite fierce and most of the employees were quite frightened of him, but he was also very much respected.

Academic: My Degree Subjects

My subjects were Social Anthropology, Economic History, Bantu Law and Administration and African Languages (Sesotho). I was lucky to have Dr Isaac Schapera as my Social Anthropology lecturer. He wrote many books on the Southern Bantu and was a good friend of my father's.

In my second year at university Dr Schapera accompanied Dad on a trip into Bechuanaland for ten days visiting various tribal areas and because it was university holidays, Dad took me along. I got to know Professor Schapera well socially as a result of this trip. My lecturer in Bantu Law and Administration was Dr Jack Simons who was classified by some experts as one of the ten most dangerous Communists in Southern Africa. At that stage he was still permitted to lecture but in the 1950s the South African Government banned him and he lost his job at the university. I always found him totally fair in his lectures. He certainly never tried to put across a strong Communist line and I didn't think he sounded at all dangerous when lecturing to us students.

My Sesotho lecturer was Dr A.C. Jordan, from the Transkei, an African. In 1949 when I was at university, and for that matter for the full three years that I was there, the Government still allowed non-white students to attend Cape Town University and sit in the same classrooms as whites. It was only in subsequent years that the Government started up segregated universities with a requirement that you attended a university of your own ethnic group. In Bantu Law and Administration and Social Anthropology about half the class was non-white. Although those students attended lectures with us they were not permitted to attend social functions, live in the university residences or participate in university sport.

Dad Dies Suddenly

I learnt of Dad's death when I bought a newspaper to read on the bus after a game of golf. The article was on the front page. No one from our family had contacted me.

After the mid-year holidays spent in Mafeking with Mum and Dad, Gerald and I had gone back to university a few days later. We knew Dad was not well. About ten days after our return to university, during the week I went to play golf at the Mowbray Golf Course, catching buses there and back. On the return trip I bought a newspaper and there on the front page was a picture of Dad with the caption "Senior British Official Dies". On page 2 there was a half-page obituary.

I went back to university and phoned Gerald who had also seen the paper. We did not go home for the funeral. Apparently my uncle, who had gone with my mother when Dad was taken by ambulance to hospital in Johannesburg from Mafeking, had forgotten to send us a telegram or phone us.

In those days there were no British Colonial Service pensions and Mum was left not well off at all. It was ironic because Dad had worked for the previous couple of years to bring in a pension scheme and about a year later it came into effect but there was no retrospectivity. All Dad got for forty years service was a £3,000 annuity which was paid to Mum. Having been in the Colonial Service all his working life the family owned no home and therefore Mum was left without a home to move into and very little money.

Gerald at this stage had six months to go at university. He subsequently admitted to me that he had intended failing so that he could have another year at university so that he and Sharkey King could carry on their antics for a while longer. To his credit, he got down to his studies and passed everything.

Gerald in cricketing gear.

I had eighteen months to go and I desperately wanted to complete my university degree. There was some resistance from other members of the family to allowing me to stay on but Mum insisted that £750 of her £3,000 annuity must be handed over to me in cash in a lump sum and that I was to ensure that I completed my university studies, but I must pay for all my own expenses from that annuity. I successfully completed my university years and have always been eternally grateful to Mum for what she did because my life would have been very different had she not ensured that I completed my studies.

Fate Robbed Me in a Cruel Way

I have always felt that fate was very cruel to me in that I had just established a bond with Dad, which promised so much for the future, when he was taken away.

In 1950 I was in my second year at Cape Town University and went home to Mafeking for the four-week July vacation. Dad was into his second year as Acting Resident Commissioner and still not confirmed to the substantive position. I have written elsewhere about this particular issue, which is a story in itself. Poor Dad looked worn out what with his membership of the Royal Commission chaired by Sir Walter Harrigan with the task of coming up with recommendations on the course of action appropriate to sort out the Seretse Khama affair (I have written at length on this latter issue which had serious potential implications for British-South African political relations). To add to his troubles, his 84-year-old mother had recently had a serious heart attack and clung to life by a thread.

It was the last few days of my holidays and Dad asked me if I would accompany him on an official trip to Lobatsi which would entail no more than 100 miles each way. I welcomed the invitation. We sat together in the rear seat of the chauffer-driven black Jaguar. I remember it all so well because it was the first time Dad had talked to me man to man about the official side of what he was doing. I was very flattered and it was a great bonding experience. On the trip home the discussion continued. That night I went to dinner, which was quite formal. Dad sat at the head of the table to seat twelve, my mother seated on his right and me on his left. The waiter in his starched white suit and white gloves brought in a leg of roast lamb and placed it on the serving table and then looked at Dad as if to say, can you please do the carving. Instead, Dad told him to call Temami, our cook of 30 years, and ask him to carve. This done, the waiter took the dish of carved meat and the three separate vegetable dishes to each person in turn to choose their own serving. At one awful point, the waiter dropped some cutlery on the wooden table and it made a lot of noise. Dad admonished him loudly in Sechuana. Poor man, his hands shook thereafter. My mother and I held our breath for the rest of the meal but it passed without further incident. Dad spoke little. It was obvious that his thoughts and worries at that moment were elsewhere,

The following night I caught the train back to Cape Town to continue my studies. I was sorry to go but I had the feeling that a bond between Dad and I was lying there in waiting to be built on and strengthened with the passing of the years. It was a great feeling.

As I have already written, the week after I returned to University I had an afternoon free of lectures so I caught the bus to the Mowbray golf course and played 18 holes. In those days Cape Town had two daily newspapers – "The Cape Times" in the morning and "The Cape Argus" in the afternoon. As I got onto the bus for the return trip to my university residence I bought a newspaper, opened it and there on the front page was a picture of Dad with the caption "Senior British Official Dies". No one at home had contacted me.

Dad's knowledge of Botswana in every aspect was vast. As I edit and read his diaries, I so often say to myself, "If only you were here, what a stunning story we could make of this."

Mum has Facial Surgery for Cancer

A matter of months after Dad died, Mum developed cancer in the upper lip. She went down to Cape Town and the specialist surgeon insisted that surgery was necessary. He was a well-known South African surgeon called Dr Penn, renowned for his work on the faces of Air Force personnel during the war. I believe he used Mum as a guinea pig because he offered to do the operation at no cost but said that he would perform a new procedure. He cut away most of the upper lip then took flesh from below the bottom and twisted it up into the gap. Her mouth was completely sealed for six weeks and she drank out of a straw. It was in fact a graft from the one section into the other.

The graft didn't take, went septic and Mum was left deformed for the rest of her life. She had been a good-looking woman and it must have been extremely hard for her to find herself in a situation where she was no longer the First Lady of the community and at the same time had to front up to people with a facial deformity.

Gerald and I saw quite a lot of Mum when she came down to Cape Town after Dad had died and before she went in for surgery. Gerald was very good for her because he continued to be cheerful and fool around. I can well remember on one occasion, which would not have been more than a few weeks after Dad had died, his saying to Mum that he was arranging a seance for that evening so that Mum could communicate with Dad and just find out how he was doing. It was good for her to have someone like him, always cheerful and always funny but at the same time a very nice person.

It was also very good for me after Dad died to continue at university surrounded by my friends. I was always busy and there was no time to become morbid. It would have been horrible to have been stranded in Mafeking doing some dull job and living a long way away from all my good university friends. So I took an extra two subjects to make three, all of which I passed with ease.

I played all the season for the Under 19 A University Team and scored many tries and thoroughly enjoyed my rugby. At the end of the year I found myself with one single subject to do in my third year to get my degree. I went back to Mafeking and by this stage Mum was living in a house in Mafeking which she shared with Granny Minchin. This gave Spencer the freedom to use the family home as he pleased, which must have made Spencer's life a great deal easier in so far as his social life was concerned.

Holiday Job in Gaborone
Cycling at night through the bush with a torch

For the greater part of the Christmas holidays I worked at Gaborone — about one hundred and sixty kilometres north of Mafeking — as a Clerk in the Public Works Department office. I boarded with Mr Wright who was a jailer. For weekends I took a train from Gaborone to Mafeking. When I had to return, my usual procedure was to catch the mixed goods train from Mafeking to Gaborone on Sunday evening. The train left Mafeking at 8pm and I would put my bicycle into the guard's van and establish myself in one of the compartments in the passenger section. Generally the train consisted of about thirty goods carriages and one passenger carriage. The train stopped at every single little siding and would get into Gaborone about 1am. I would get my bicycle out of the luggage van and ride the eight kilometres through the bush on a bumpy gravel road to the Wright residence near the jail. On moonlit nights I could see where I was going but on dark nights I would use a torch held in one hand.

It is quite interesting to think back that I didn't have the slightest fear about riding through the bush on my own and where that riding took place nearly fifty years ago there is now the capital city of Bechuanaland with a population of 100,000.

I had quite a good social time in Gaborone. The Wrights had a daughter who was about fifteen years old but I can't say that she ever raised any enthusiasm in me. There were a number of families who I had known for many years living in Gaborone and they often invited me round for a meal. Then there was always the train journey on Friday evening back to Mafeking and I would join up with my university friends there and we always had a good time.

One Subject to go

At the beginning of 1951 I went back to university and although I only needed one subject for my degree I decided to take three subjects just to keep myself busy. I was still in Smuts Hall with all my friends and we had a staircase right in the corner of the first quadrangle. My room, E14, overlooked a wonderful view of the Cape Flats and the mountains in the background. It was a happy year with lots of social activity and I once again played for the University Under 19 A Team and was also picked for the Combined Universities Under 19 Team. We played the "rest" and had a convincing win.

New Job — Didn't Last Long!

At the end of 1951, I once again passed all subjects and got my degree, Bachelor of Arts. I was very envious of so many of my friends who were doing Law and Medicine and Architecture and so on because they had another two years to go at university. However, I had my degree and I had to leave. I said goodbye to everyone and off I went to Mafeking. I was still only nineteen.

Mum got me a job in the Bechuanaland Government in Mahalapye. I stayed at the Mahalapye Hotel and worked in the Public Works Department as a Clerk on a lousy pay, staying in a lousy hotel in a dusty village. I occasionally went down to Mafeking to see Mum but for the most part stayed in Mahalapye, played cricket for the local team and was kindly treated by a number of families I knew. There was no golf course. The main entertainment was provided by the passenger trains between South Africa and Rhodesia which used to come through Mahalapye. The engines had a pull of eight hundred kilometres from Mafeking to Bulawayo and in Mahalapye the train stopped for fifty minutes whilst the engine stocked up on coal and water and got itself greased again and so on. This provided the opportunity for everyone on the train to get out and stretch their legs. The Mahalapye Hotel was slap on the station and the bar in fact opened from the platform. There were a lot of blue gums to one side of the hotel and a little circular concrete dance floor with an African band. Mahalapye was well known by those who travelled regularly on the train through Bechuanaland Protectorate for the fifty-minute stop with the band and a couple of quick beers. When you had been on the train for a long time it was a great opportunity to just stretch for a while and relax. I used to watch out for people I knew on the train and it's amazing how often there was someone who you could relate to and talk to.

The worst time was in late February when the train had all my university friends on it returning from their Christmas holidays in Rhodesia. My gosh, how I wished that I could hop on the train and go down to Cape Town and back to university with them.

What I did on a couple of occasions was to hop onto the train that went thorugh Mahalapye in the early evening and spend a couple of hours going south with them. We generally had a bit of a party in the dining saloon and then about two in the morning our passenger train would cross with the mixed goods train coming up from Mafeking and I would hop off the passenger train, probably at Lobatsi, and get into the mixed goods which had one passenger carriage on it. I would then get back to Mahalapye about six in the morning in time for a wash and to go off for work. It was a fairly exhausting night but I used to thoroughly enjoy it.

King George VI Dies

It's funny how when one thinks back on a particular place one can relate it to the big historical events. My recollection of Mahalapye was when King George VI died. In those days the monarchy was prominent in the affections and lives of citizens of the British Empire and everyone was really shocked. He died in his late fifties and was a relatively young man, so his death came as an unexpected event.

Recollections of Where you were When Great Historical Events Occur

The other recollections I have of historical events associated with places was when I was District Commissioner in Mokhotlong in Lesotho in 1962 and the Cuban missile crisis was on the boil. John Kennedy was President of the United States and Khrushchev was in charge in Russia and there was this great stand-off. Castro had set up a Communist government in Cuba, less than one hundred miles offshore from the US, and Russia had despatched a convoy of ships bound for Cuba with a cargo of surface-to-surface missiles which were to be deployed in Cuba aimed at the USA. I remember walking back home from the office in the middle of the morning to listen to the radio to find out what had happened and hearing that Khrushchev had backed down and ordered the ships home in the face of an American naval armada sent out to intercept them.

The other big historical event occurred in 1967 when Gail and I were on a Rhine cruise from Basel to Rotterdam. We were just reaching Cologne when we heard that Bobby Kennedy had been assassinated. We had a lot of Americans on board and there was utter devastation among them. Americans were still hurting from the assassination of John Kennedy in 1963.

There are other events of importance which I remember well and associate with particular places but I won't go into all those details. It's probably worth a mention that I still regard the two Kennedy brothers as the greatest orators I have ever listened to. Both had the charisma and the eloquence to stir my thoughts and passions. I remember when Bobby Kennedy visited South Africa in 1967 he made a number of speeches which I found quite stirring.

Mahalapye Misery

Back to Mahalapye and my misery. The Mahalapye Hotel is right on the railway station so I often went down to the station when a passenger train was due. Trains stopped for 45 minutes to enable the engine to be oiled and greased and to take on more coal. One night I was sitting on the verandah of the pub overlooking the Mahalapye Station and I looked up and in the corner of my eye, there coming down the wall not more than about six inches from my head, was a scorpion as big as one's hand and dark black. I didn't know scorpions were able to crawl up walls but I moved off that bench very quickly. I guess it might have been one of the deciding factors but over the next couple of weeks I decided Mahalapye was not the place for me despite the fact that Mum thought I should become a hardworking young man in Bechuanaland. I didn't tell Mum until everything had been organised; I resigned my job, packed my bags and went down to Mafeking for three or four days and then straight back to Cape Town.

Back to Cape Town

When I got to Cape Town I was back with all my friends. Basil Bennets, John Naude, "Puck" Addison and Greg Forsythe got together and lived in a double-storey thatched cottage in Wynberg and I was able to join them. It was a beautiful little cottage with a nice garden and we were able to afford a maid to look after us — to do our cooking and washing and cleaning whilst we concentrated on our studies! The others were all full time at university — Basil and John doing law, "Puck" commerce and Greg architecture — but I signed on for one half subject in Native Administration which made me eligible to play rugby for the university.

These cottages had, for hundreds of years, been occupied by coloured families but the Nationalist Government in South Africa had brought in the Group Areas Act which required that people of different races be residentially segregated and it was determined that Wynberg should be a White area. The Coloured families who had occupied cottages in Wynberg such as our cottage — Campview — were moved off and resettled on the windy Cape Flats. It is greatly to my shame that at that time the political aspects of how Basil had acquired Campview and the unfairness with which the previous occupants had been treated never entered my thoughts. I guess as a privileged white we simply enjoyed everything to the full and to the total exclusion of fairness to non-whites. In fact, we were cloned into our beliefs of white superiority.

And then it was time to go out and find a job. The tobacco companies had a reputation for employing people with some sort of sporting prowess and Mr Berger, who was in charge of the United Tobacco Company office in the city, fortunately remembered me from a couple of good games I had played for the university in the Under 19 Team on Newlands. He employed me as a clerk and no doubt he expected me to do great things on the rugby field. As it turned out, my rugby expectations were not fulfilled because I was only in the University First Team, off and on, and I don't think I performed particularly well.

John Naude and I shared a Hillman car — the 1936 Hillman which cost us fifty pounds each — and when I look back on some of the things I did in that car I get cold shivers down my back. For four weeks it had a dead battery and I used to park it on a hill every night and run it down the hill to start it and I drove through rush hour traffic in Cape Town every day for those six weeks. We couldn't afford a new battery.

Fortunately it never stalled or needed to be restarted because the battery just did not build up any charge at all. I think of the potential to be sitting on De Waal Drive in the five o'clock traffic stalled in the middle of the road. In those days De Waal Drive was simply an ordinary winding road, one lane in each direction. Today it has three lanes in each direction.

The five of us got on well together. We had some great parties in our Wynberg cottage. Wine could be bought for five shillings a gallon and a big bottle of beer cost ten pence so the alcohol side was not too much of a problem from an expense point of view. Our maid was a good cook and Basil Bennets in particular was a very social person and insisted on maintaining high standards in the cottage — he never allowed us to be too untidy. He subsequently bought the eight-storey Elizabeth Hotel at Sea Point on the foreshore and looked after it himself for many years. It was a multistorey complex with a very high reputation.

I guess it would be quite funny to tell the story of Basil's first seduction. It's necessary to put things into the context of the times because in my university days there was no pill available for birth control so we were sexually far less active than the modern generation. One night Basil came back at midnight with a lady whose name I well remember but will not record, but I will note that she was a university student and not particularly attractive — but buxom. Basil took her into his bedroom and he knew that the rest of us would be intrigued as to what was going on and might well spy on him, so I remember the shifting of furniture as he pushed his wardrobe across the door so none of us could see what was going on.

Basil was in love with Adele Jooste. They went out together for years but she married someone else while he was overseas. Basil remained a bachelor until Adele was widowed thirty years later. They married soon after her husband died.

During that season I went on tour with the university rugby team. We toured the South Western Districts of the Cape Province and played four matches at places like Oudtshoorn and Mossel Bay. It was a very enjoyable tour and it was good to be with all those well known and established rugby players and me still very much the junior, but I got three out of the four games and performed reasonably well.

At the end of 1952 I took up a position in Lesotho and so ended my enjoyable days at Campview. Basil continued to live at Campview for many years and, as mentioned, became a big property owner in the area with his Elizabeth Hotel purchase.

When I visited Cape Town in 2005 for Tracy's wedding we went to find Campview. The area is now known as Little Chelsea, with lots of fascinating white-walled thatched cottages.

Farewell to Varsity Days

In September of that year, 1952, the rugby season was nearly over and I didn't enjoy my job. Just before Dad died I had a talk to him about my future job prospects. It had always been assumed that I would join the British Colonial Service just as Dad had done and my grandfather before him. I said to Dad that I was no longer certain that I wanted to join the Colonial Service and he said, "Well that's entirely up to you but I do strongly advise you to finish your university degree and then decide what employment you want to take up." I was in some doubt for a long time as to what I wanted to do but having spent that winter in Cape Town and with the summer coming up and all the circumstances surrounding it I decided that the Colonial Service was what I really did want to do.

A Chance Meeting that Shaped my Entire Life

It was an amazing coincidence that when I was making up my mind on this issue I happened to sit down on a park bench in the Cape Town Botanical Gardens to eat my fish and chips at lunch time. I was still employed by the United Tobacco Company at the time. A man came and sat next to me and said, "You're Nettelton, aren't you?" I replied that I was. He said, "Do you still want to join the Colonial Service?" and I said, "Yes, I do." So he said, "I knew your father well and I suggest that you come to the British High Commission Office and see me. Just give my secretary a ring and arrange a time."

He happened to be the Deputy British High Commissioner in South Africa and a short time later he was appointed as Governor of British Borneo. His name was Sir Charles Robinson. Anyway I went to see him and he explained that as I was only twenty I was not eligible for employment within the administration of the British Colonial Service (until I was twenty-two) but he would find me a clerical job in Basutoland if I wished. I said I would like to take up such an appointment and three weeks later I was on the train on my way to Basutoland, which of course is now called Lesotho.

Travelling on that train was an old experience for me and at Beaufort West which the train reached about nine in the morning, I got out to stretch my legs and I met a guy on the platform also stretching his legs. By huge coincidence it turned out that he was also on his way to Basutoland to take up a new job. His name was Rupert Langerman and when we got to Maseru in Basutoland we found ourselves occupying rondavel/bedroom accommodation right alongside one another. Rupert has remained a friend of mine throughout my life.

Cambridge University

Boat Voyage from Capetown to Southampton, Train to Cambridge

I left for the United Kingdom in September 1954 on a Union Castle boat, the Sterling Castle. The ship would have carried about three hundred passengers and of those at least two hundred were students going to various universities in the United Kingdom. There would have been at least sixty of us going to either Oxford or Cambridge. We had a great social time on the boat but there were not nearly enough girls to go around. The girls that there were seemed to have this female fascination for officers in uniform, so we had our own fun without girls. We participated in sporting events such as the deck tennis and enjoyed that. The sea voyages between Cape Town and the UK were such an established part of the South African way of life that it was sad to ultimately see air travel take over and the sea liners disappear. The Union Castle mail ship left Cape Town at four o'clock every Friday afternoon, fifty-two weeks a year and the ships were always well booked. It was a ten-day voyage and this was just long enough. The great plus for such voyages was that you were on the ship because you were going to some definite destination usually with a particular purpose but that interlude of ten days on the sea was always a great social event and most relaxing. Cruise liners are quite different.

The departure from Cape Town had its comical moments. I can remember on some occasion standing on the docks next to a guy who was farewelling a girlfriend. They were waving to one another and she was on the ship and calling out to him, "You will write? You won't forget to write soon? Oh, how I'm going to miss you," and he was responding in the appropriate manner and then as the ship pulled further away he turned to the male friend next to him and said, "Thank Christ she's gone."

Meet Robin Cherry – A Very Good Friend at Cambridge

Robin Cherry with his wife, Helen, and daughter, Janet

It was on this voyage that I met Robin Cherry who was also going to Cambridge. He was a brilliant physicist who subsequently worked closely with Dr Christiaan Barnard doing laboratory work in the lead-up to the world's first heart transplant which was carried out at the Groote Schuur Hospital in Cape Town in the early 1960s.

Robin travelled with Dr Barnard on several trips to the USA. Robin was at Cambridge University with Friedel Sellschop, who was a member of our group at Cambridge, and Freidel was subsequently right at the centre of the development of the South African armaments program in the 1960s. Robin was, I know, approached by Friedel to join his working group in South Africa and Robin's wife Helen tells of how Robin at that time used to go off to the Muizenberg Beach and walk for hours trying to sort out the moral issues between his conscience and the excitement of being associated with new projects. He eventually declined to join Friedel and became a Lecturer in Physics at Cape Town University and subsequently became Dean of the Faculty of Science. Robin was subsequently enticed into a physics research program by the French Government and was based at Majorca in the Mediterranean.

Robin, quite ironically, had known Gail all his life but when Robin and I met on the Sterling Castle on the way to England, I didn't know Gail. Robin was in the same party as myself at the Cambridge May Ball in 1955 – this was at Pembroke College. The following year Gail was Robin's partner at the Pembroke College May Ball.

Three years later Gail and I met and in talking we realised that we had been just one year apart at Cambridge. Gail tells of how she was in a bookstore in London when Robin appeared around the corner and of course they had known one another for a long time and he threw his arms around her and said, "Will you come to the May Ball with me?" No sensible unattached girl would ever turn down an invitation to either an Oxford or Cambridge May Ball and of course she accepted, although she admitted that in Pretoria she had always disliked Robin because he was just too clever. In later years Robin became godfather to our second daughter.

Union Castle liner leaving Cape Town.

When we arrived in Southhampton we took the train up to London, about one and half hour's journey, and were met at the station by Dennis Robinson and Ian Reeler. It was nice to be met in London by old friends and we spent that night at a bed and breakfast. In those days the London bed and breakfasts cost 12/6 (twelve shillings and sixpence) and you got a really good breakfast for that price. The next day I went up to Cambridge and Dennis and Ian went back to Oxford accompanied by a couple of other guys on the ship who were going to Oxford and who had been known to them.

Queens Becomes my College at Cambridge

At Cambridge I was put into Queens' College, famous for Isaac Newton and the Elizabethan Tudor Court. I had my own rooms in the Fisher Building. To get to my rooms I walked across the "mathematical" bridge over the Cam River every day of my life. One is immediately absorbed into the atmosphere of a university like Cambridge. You are surrounded by history and tradition and culture and learning and it really is a great atmosphere.

My rooms in Fisher Building consisted of a small flat with my own bathroom, sitting room and bedroom with cooking facilities. The sitting room had big windows which looked out across the River Cam with St Catherine's Cottage on the right, then Kings College Chapel and beyond that Trinity College. It was a magnificent view and one of the greatest recollections I have was waking up on a cold January morning and looking out of the window to find the snow had fallen

Beautiful Cambridge. Kings College Chapel and various colleges.

softly during the night and was hanging on the trees and on the grass and on the roofs and there was a misty sun breaking through. It was a really beautiful sight. I ate my meals in the college hall which was a typical Tudor room with long tables and benches and you just sat wherever you could find a place. We were still in an era when we had to wear academic gowns after dinner if we went out. The Bulldogs (university police) roamed the streets and if you were found wandering around not wearing your academic gowns you could be fined. The college gates closed at varying times. I was lucky in that the Queens' College gates were endowed by some former benefactor and this endowment enabled the gates to stay open an additional hour. I guess the endowment went towards paying the wages of the gate attendant for an extra hour every night. If you did arrive late you had to pay a fine to gain entry back into your college. One soon learns the tricks of the trade and on a number of occasions as I became more confident and found myself out at some function pretty late at night I learned how to hang onto the spiked rails over a tributary of the Cam and hand over hand get myself across the water and into the College grounds. I did this little exercise many times and became quite expert at it.

Early Lesson — Do not Drink Cider at 9.30 in the Morning!

On my first day of studies at Cambridge I went to a lecture at 8.45am and sat next to a person called Ian Butler. He was, of course, also studying for the Administration of the British Colonial Service and subsequently went to the Gilbert and Ellis Islands. He was an Oxford graduate and had been the Oxford University Heavy Weight Boxing Champion. He was an awfully nice guy. At the end of the lecture, which would have been about 9.30 in the morning, Ian suggested that we go to the Old Mill for a cider. I had not had breakfast but it was my first day at lectures and here was Ian, an old hand in the university business of England, so who was I to refuse? The Old Mill is on the River Cam. Ian and I went down to the pub where we each bought a pint of Merrydown Cider and sat down at a table overlooking the beautiful scene of the weir and the river and the green fields beyond. It was really rather lovely.

The big problem was that I didn't understand that Merrydown Cider is the strongest cider you can get in England and it has the effect of going to your knees. Bearing in mind the fact that I had had no breakfast, I found that by the time we had finished our pint of cider and were due to return to the next lecture, which was at 10.30, my knees were a bit wobbly. Ian laughed but it didn't seem to affect him at all. I got to my lecture but I must admit I'm a little bit hazy on what the lecturer said. From that day on I was very wary of Merrydown Cider, in fact I was wary of cider in all its different brand names. It does seem to go to your knees whereas a lot of the other alcoholic drinks have the effect of going to your head.

We often went punting on the River Cam.

Above: Tudor Court, Queens College
Left: Entrance to Queen College where I was a student.

The so called "Mathematical" bridge over the River Cam which is part of Queen's College. It was not designed by Newton as myth would have it.

Fisher Building where I had rooms. One of the Queen's College residential facilities situated on the River Cam just across the "Mathematical" bridge from the main college buildings.

The Atmosphere of Cambridge Stimulates a Quest for Knowledge

Back to Cambridge. None of my twenty-three Colonial Service compatriots were in Queens' College with me. Particularly in the evenings my social activities were mainly associated with friends drawn from my own college and also a Rhodesian and South African contingent who I had known previously and who were dotted around various colleges at Cambridge. After dinner it was a normal procedure to go out somewhere for coffee and the conversation at these little social gatherings was always quite stimulating. Looking back at those times, I realise that I was surrounded by very clever men, many of whom were to make a considerable mark in their areas of study in the broader community in the future. The intellect and knowledge and the breadth of that knowledge and the articulate manner in which they could argue a point was all very stimulating and you felt that you also wanted to be part of that intellect and quest for knowledge and expressing opinions and arguing and so on. At Cambridge there were a huge variety of societies and organisations that students belonged to. I remember I always used to laugh at one of the societies which was formed when I was there under the name of "Society for the Abolition of Smog". In actual fact whoever got that society going really had a good perspective on what was to come because it was the forerunner for a better understanding of the need to control pollution. In 1954 in cities such as London one still experienced those famous 'pea soup' fogs which were partly a natural fog and mainly smoke from the many belching industrial chimneys in the Greater London area.

A Debate in the Cambridge Union Centred on Human Rights in South Africa and Rhodesia (1954)

A couple of us went regularly to listen to the debates at the Cambridge Union. The Cambridge Union and the Oxford Union are famous for the quality of debate and are known as the training ground for many of the politicians and orators of the future in the United Kingdom, and as it was in those days, the British Dominions. I remember one debate in particular centred on human rights and the situation in South Africa and Rhodesia. The issue centred on the evolving apartheid form of government in South Africa and the Colonialist attitudes in Rhodesia. At that stage in my life I was quite sympathetic towards the rights of non-whites but thought in a rather old-fashioned way in that we, the whites, knew how to govern so much better than the non-whites. I was never a person who was pro-apartheid and when in South Africa I was often very critical of the South African Government, but when I found myself in a different environment in England with very critical attitudes towards South Africa and Rhodesia — often, I felt, based on only part understanding of the reality of the situation — I tended to argue the South African/Rhodesian point of view.

When I look back on that era of my thinking, which is more than fifty years ago, I can understand that my views were born from those of my peers around me. Situations such as this can probably be judged in the perspective of the era in which you live. Perspectives change and all these years later I could never countenance the views that I held then, but I don't criticise myself too much because I realise that I was living according to the dictates of my time and I was not the sort of person who was a radical and prepared to stick my neck out and break new political ground. South Africa in that era was a land flowing with milk and honey for a white person so long as you did not break the rules. For those who tried to break out of the set parameters the penalties were extremely severe and I just was not interested in getting myself into a lot of political trouble, as happened to some of my friends. The daughter of my good friend Robin Cherry, aged twenty-two and a newly graduated teacher, was put in custody for two years with strict limits on visits by friends and family.

Back to the debate about human rights as it affected South Africa and Rhodesia at that time. A group of us went to the debate at the Cambridge Union. We were all from South Africa or Rhodesia and I was from Botswana and now working in Lesotho. We cheered our debating team who endeavoured to put across the complexity of the situation in Southern Africa and explained that at that particular time it was necessary to proceed cautiously with long-term objectives in mind which would eventually allow the non-white to attain equal political and economic rights. Looking back on it, I realise that the political masters of the time had no intention of granting that equality inside five hundred years. Apartheid was born out of economic domination and supremacy which directed the majority of the wealth into the pockets of the whites, with the non-whites performing the hard grind and hard labour. In the mid-1950s there were approximately thirty million Africans in South Africa, plus one million Indians, two million mixed race and five million whites. The economic wealth was divided with one half of the cake going to the whites to share amongst five million people and the other half going to the other thirty million to share amongst themselves. The outcome was an extremely prosperous and cushy life for whites. When in political control and enjoying such a comfortable and affluent existence, how many men and women either white or black would not fight to preserve their way of life? There are many parallels which still exist in other countries, particularly South America.

Back to the Cambridge Union. I can't remember who won the debate but it was a good rowdy evening and we enjoyed ourselves. No doubt after the debate we went off and had coffee and probably ended up talking about the forthcoming rugby match between England and the Springboks or our next trip across to the Continent and by the time we went to bed, we had probably forgotten about the debate.

What I did Academically at Cambridge

My main subject at Cambridge was Criminal Law because as a District Officer I would be required to assume the duties of a Magistrate in the District in which I worked. I did well in the subject. I really did work hard at it. My other main subject should have been Sesotho because that is the language of Basutoland and all of the twenty-three others on the course were required to do an intense study of the language of the country to which we were going. Unfortunately there was nobody to teach this language. To the credit of the British Government they placed huge importance on the ability of the District Officer to be able to communicate with the local people in their own language.

When I got back to Basutoland I was required to pass certain language exams and if I did not do so the incremental rises in my salary that would normally take place automatically each year would be suspended until those exams had been passed. Likewise with law: I had to pass exams when I got back to Basutoland in criminal, civil and statutory law and until I had passed those exams my increments were withheld.

I was in an unusual position in regard to language because I had done Sesotho as one of my Cape Town University subjects and there just didn't seem to be anyone around to teach me. Eventually they found a Mr Sillery who had at one time been Resident Commissioner in Bechuanaland and had worked with Dad. He was one of these academic linguists. We agreed after two or three lessons that there really was not much point in pursuing the classes. This left me with a lot of extra time on my hands.

We also did a lot of study on anthropology, road surveying and elementary bridge building, conflict resolution and economics and a multitude of subjects which tied up into a very useful course which I enjoyed.

I Am Proud of the British Colonial Service and the Work We Did

The course at Cambridge was a precursor to twenty-five years in the British Colonial Service and I found what I did rewarding and enjoyable. Our Colonial Service group consisted of twenty-three men. We were destined to go to all corners of the world. One must bear in mind the fact that in 1954 one third of the world came in some form or other under British orbit. At school one had these maps of the world with the areas of political influence marked in different colours and the British Empire was always in red and you looked at the map and that one third of the world just stood out so markedly.

To illustrate a point, of the twenty-three, the varied future work destinations — just to name some — were Hong Kong, Sierra Leone, Tanganyika, Kenya, Uganda, Swaziland, Gambia, Basutoland, Bechuanaland Protectorate, Gilbert and Ellis Islands, Belize, British Guiana, Seychelles, Sudan, Ghana, Aden.

The places the people were going to straddled the world. It really was quite exciting. I had the advantage of having spent eighteen months in Basutoland working in a clerical situation and also I had grown up in Bechuanaland and my father had been a senior official in the administration of that country. That gave me a great advantage in my studies at Cambridge and also in the relationship with my fellow students because most of them, in fact all of them, had never lived or worked outside the United Kingdom and what they were going to was a completely new environment. I already knew that environment and I knew what I was going to and this gave me a great advantage over my fellow students. In those days the Raj still reigned supreme and we all had great pride in the British Empire and we felt privileged that we were being trained to go and work in the colonies and to be part of the Raj; in fact a great British tradition.

The administration of the British Colonial Service had a great tradition of integrity and after working for fifteen years as part of the British Colonial Service I finally departed feeling proud of what we had done and achieved in the colonies and territories. When independence finally came to those many colonies, we left an administration that worked and which had the trust of the local community, there was an infrastructure of roads, there were hospitals in all the major centres which functioned efficiently with nurses and doctors, there was an education system which could boast (certainly in Basutoland where I served) that every child had an opportunity to learn how to read and write, there were judicial systems which were not corrupt and the police were likewise administered by white officers, none of whom in my fifteen years in Basutoland I would ever have considered to be corrupt.

I'll talk more about this particular subject later in these memoirs but when I look at Africa today and its problems, I believe that history will judge the British Colonial Service kindly, but it will not be put into its true perspective for quite a long time to come. The main reason for this is the fact that the British and other European powers' involvement in Africa started predominantly with the slave trade and that white over black domination aspect extended into the Colonial era. This should not have been the case because the Colonial era was vastly different to that of the slave trade, which was formally abolished by Britain in 1836 as a result of the efforts of William Wilberforce and Sir Spencer Perceval, PM of Britain 1809-1812.

Cambridge Academic System

The Duchess of Alba as painted by Goya. I thought she was so beautiful that she adorned my bedroom wall for the duration of my stay at Cambridge. My interest in art was at that time considerable and the Cambridge environment stimulated it further. In 1954 when I visited Spain with Rupert, we spent time in the Madrid art gallery which has a superb collection of Goya's art, including this portrait of the Duchess of Alba, who became Goya's mistress. He painted her nude and then the Duke (her husband) asked to see the portrait so he hurriedly had to paint some clothes on her!

At Oxford and Cambridge the university system is based very much on the tutorial. One of the reasons why those two universities are so expensive to attend is that you have a tutor and you meet with that tutor many times during the week and spend many hours with him and by the end of the year he or she has a very good idea as to what your genuine academic worth is. The emphasis is simply not on exams. You write exams, but in the event of doing poorly in that exam the matter is referred to your tutor and the tutor is a big factor as to whether you're worth a pass or not, and at what level. The tutor will often advise you as to which lectures to attend and could well say, 'don't go to so and so's lectures, he's not particularly good, I would go to such and such'.

One of the requirements to attain your pass is to be able to establish that you have eaten sixty dinners at Cambridge for the term. The academic year consists of three terms, each of sixty days and if you have not eaten your sixty dinners for each of those three terms, you are not in statu pupillari and you are therefore not eligible to be awarded a degree.

One of the real positives for me was that I was able to get a far better understanding of the English public school system (which in Australia would be private school) and its demeanour and attitudes and approach to things. I openly admit that before going to Cambridge, I had found quite intimidating the ultra self-confident and articulate demeanour of the English public schools and unique university products who were so often those serving in the administration of the British Colonial Service. I felt a bit inferior because they were a majority and they had a common background and they were always so darned confident.

After a year at Cambridge I found I had gained a great deal of additional self-confidence and no longer regarded the English public school products as being some elite group superior to myself. I got on well with them and I got to like them but they were always still a group on their own and with my background I was never quite allowed into the club: I was a "Colonial boy". But on the other hand to their credit I never felt downgraded and inferior and as things turned out, in many respects I knew that I outperformed a lot of them.

Christmas Holidays Skiing in Austria

In that first term I did all the usual things such as punting on the River Cam with my friends and drinking lots of coffee at various restaurants and eating many Indian curries because the cheapest and best food in the restaurants was to be had at the Indian restaurants which were quite numerous in Cambridge. I played rugby for the college and enjoyed it and I got on well with my friends and it was a really good term.

Then the first holidays came around. We had three weeks off from about two weeks before Christmas and went back to university in the second week of January. I stayed on at university for the first week and one of the memorable occasions was going to the Kings College Chapel to hear the Vienna Boys Choir singing. I find choral singing in those old English cathedrals a very moving experience and I really did enjoy that particular concert.

For ten days before Christmas I joined the combined Oxford-Cambridge skiing tour to Zurs in Austria and we had a great time. Zurs is a little village in the Vorarlberg of Austria and the entire village was taken over by the Oxford-Cambridge group with their friends and girlfriends and so on. We had ten glorious days in perfect conditions. I had never skied before but by the end I was thoroughly enjoying it. There is nothing more exhilarating than schussing down a really steep slope with the wind whistling past your ears and knowing you're going really fast and if you fall

Skiing at Zurs in Austria, 1954. A combined Cambridge/Oxford student party took over the whole village for ten days.

you're going to really hurt yourself. It's very exciting. In the evenings there was much festivity and usually we got to bed about 2.00am. Somehow it was possible to be up again at nine o'clock and on the slopes and off skiing again. The mountain air is so exhilarating and you never seem to get tired.

About three days before our departure I went up on a ski lift which in those days just consisted of two seats rather like a ship's anchor and one person sat on either side. When we got to the top I got off and messed around a bit and forgot to get my head out of the way, and the next seat clunked me on the back of my head. I had to have three stitches. However that didn't affect me too much. One of the pluses of that little episode was that when we went to Salzburg I had to have the stitches out and went to a doctor who, as it happened, was very interested in going to South Africa and he was full of questions about what the situation was like and wanting to know as much as I could tell him. I was with a friend called Wimpie Ahlers from South Africa and this doctor invited the two of us to join him and his wife for dinner at the Eulenspiegel which had recently been voted as one of the ten best restaurants in the world. The restaurant was within the city walls of Salzburg. It was a great meal and a great atmosphere and Wimpie and I were very glad that I had forgotten to duck and had ended up needing stitches. We felt for three stitches it was really worth it.

A Few Days in Salzburg

On Christmas Eve Wimpie and I went to a restaurant and we met some guy who maintained that he was a Russian Count who had been pushed across the border by some sort of Russian conspiracy. He said he knew Salzburg well and that he could take us to a few night spots and then to the Mass at Salzburg Cathedral at midnight. He was a pretty washed-out looking character, but he seemed to know his way around and rather suspiciously we went with him. It was most interesting going to the Mass at midnight conducted by the Bishop of Salzburg. Our so-called Count kept hiding under the seat because he said he felt that he had had a bit too much to drink and the Bishop might recognise him. It was all a bit queer but those sort of situations are quite fun.

Time with Rupert Langerman who was Living in Squalor in London

I returned to England and spent a few days in London with Rupert Langerman. He was my old friend from Maseru in Basutoland and it was great to see him again. He'd had some difficult times in London. He had this great dream that he was going to become a great author. He particularly wanted to emulate Somerset Maugham and Guy du Maupassant. He was living in some squalor in London, writing and getting all his stories rejected. He had been particularly ill and fortunately for him Ann Duncan, also from Maseru, was in London at the time and found him very ill and shipped him off to hospital with pneumonia.

He tells the story of a guy in the bed in the corner who woke up in the middle of the night with withdrawal symptoms. He must have been an alcoholic. He screamed that snakes and spiders were invading his bed. He got through that first night and the second night he stood up in bed in the middle of the night and shrieked to the rest of the ward, "I'm going to die. I'm going to die." Rupert said, "And then he laid down and died." Rupert recovered, went back to his squalor, didn't have much success in his writings so eventually got a job as a waiter. He continued in this occupation for another four or five months until he joined up with me and we went off to Spain together but I'll enlarge on that a bit later.

Second Term — Cold, Brussels Sprouts and Ice Cream

The second term at Cambridge was awfully cold. The main food in the dinner hall seemed to be Brussels sprouts, and ice cream for dessert. I have such vivid memories of those wretched Brussels sprouts and ice cream every single meal in that term. A Pakistani student in rooms close to me didn't switch his gas heater off once for the full sixty days of term and he got a bill for £300 at the end and he was absolutely devastated. I don't blame him for keeping his heater on all the time because it was darned cold.

Student Behaviour very Destructive at Times

An aspect of student behaviour at Oxford and Cambridge which I could never understand was the element of destructiveness which seemed to be part of the culture of these two universities. When I talk of destructiveness it was so often associated with sporting events. If we had a college rugby match and after that rugby match we went to our sports pavilion for a few beers, there always seemed to be some guys who thought it was imperative that they should bust the place up. So often there was damage to doors and to windows and it just was so unnecessary.

This behaviour extended into other sporting areas. A friend of mine who attended the dinner after the Oxford and Cambridge Second Rugby Teams had played said that the dinner, which was quite formal and attended by some senior persons from each university, and was held in one of the really historic dining rooms of Oxford, was highlighted by the Captain of the Oxford XV who after making his speech got on to a table (probably a fifteenth-century antique), walked down the table and poured a jug of beer over the head of the Cambridge Captain. A few glasses then got broken and there was general pandemonium but this seemed to be accepted as a normal form of behaviour at such functions. There was no disciplinary action afterwards.

I experienced the same sort of thing when I went on a three-day tour with the Queens' College rugby team down to the Southampton area and for two nights we stayed at English pubs and I found the behaviour of a group of my fellow rugby players really quite amazing. They seemed to think that it was essential to get drunk and then to behave in a thoroughly offensive way, such as urinating into the open fireplace until the fire went out. Such situations seemed to be accepted as part of the growing up process of the students and there was never any disciplinary action taken afterwards. At Cape Town University we never had any such behavioural problems. If any of our sporting teams had dared to behave in that sort of way there would have been very strong disciplinary action and I believe that the peer pressure from other students simply would not have allowed it. At Cape Town University we certainly had our hijinks but they never took on the element of destructiveness that seemed to be so pervasive at Oxford and Cambridge.

Everyone Had a Bicycle

At Cambridge the main mode of transport around the town was by bicycle. Every student had a bicycle and as a result there were literally thousands of bicycles on the streets at any time. I had my old bicycle which I bought for £4 and it carried me all over the place day and night. You never put a padlock on your bicycle and I was lucky enough not to have mine pinched but very often you found that some student was in a hurry and didn't have a bicycle and would "borrow" one from the many stacked outside every college or lecture theatre or whatever it might be, in order to get to where that person wanted to go. The bicycle would simply be left there. It was difficult to know where to look for your bike when it had been pinched.

Attitude to Sport

Another aspect of Cambridge life to which I had to adjust was the fact that in playing for the college rugby team there were never any practices — you simply pitched up on the day at the venue and you played. I had been accustomed to practising twice a week and then probably having pick-up matches in between, and as a result we were fit and we knew who we were playing with and no doubt performed a lot better for it. The attitude of so many of the students towards their sport was so very casual. It has changed now but in the mid-1950s there seemed to be a very old-fashioned casual, non-professional attitude towards sport. It was just a gentlemanly venture in which you participated almost for the fun of it and whether you did well or not did not really matter. The latter fact was a fallacy because in the UK press they longed for sporting heroes and it was quite tragic in certain instances that a sporting hero would be someone who came third. We may be criticised in Australia for being sport mad but I think it contributes a great deal to the cohesiveness of the country and also to the pride which we feel in being Australian.

My experience was in the 1950s however. Five decades later this has changed and the UK is now one of the leading sports nations in the world.

Easter Holidays in Scotland and I Meet Morag

The Easter holidays came around I went up to Edinburgh to stay with Ann Duncan, my old friend from Basutoland days. It was good to see her again. She was living in a flat fairly close to the centre of Edinburgh, one of those old grey stone buildings that will stand for ever. She shared with three others and I arrived in Edinburgh on the evening train and went straight to their flat where they happened to be having a party which was attended by about twenty young people. Ann was an only child and from a wealthy Scots family. Her father, Bill Duncan, had been an engineer in Malaysia before going out to South Africa where he and his wife, Anna, bought the Beacon Island Hotel at Plettenberg Bay. It was a beautifully located hotel and Gail and I spent our honeymoon there, but this was after Bill and Anna had moved on to other areas. The Duncans moved to Basutoland and bought the Stevens Hotel which had a very profitable liquor outlet and they must have made a fortune there. To add to the wealth of the family Anna Duncan, Ann's mother, was an only child and her parents were wealthy. He had been an engineer in Scotland and had made money. The outcome of all this was that Ann was well endowed financially and so was in a position to throw a good party.

On arrival at Ann's flat I soon got into the swing of the proceedings and it was there that I met Morag Henderson, one of Ann's flatmates. We got on extremely well and there was good chemistry between us right from the start. From that first meeting we became very close and in fact before I left England we had intentions to ultimately marry but circumstances prevented that. Morag was doing Hospital Almony (similar to social service) at Edinburgh University and was in her second year. She played hockey for Scotland and was a nice-looking girl who I must say had a lot of appeal. Over the next week I found myself being shown all the sights of Edinburgh by Morag and Ann. Edinburgh is such a beautiful city with such a feeling of maturity and solidarity — I guess just like the Scots themselves.

Hamish's Wedding in Perth — Bucks Party Stupidity

After a week in Edinburgh I went up to Perth to stay with a friend who was on the course with me at Cambridge, Hamish Robertson. Hamish was very Scots and had asked me to come to his wedding. Hamish and I shared a room in Perth and one of my recollections is of one of those awful buck's parties that men of all nationalities seem to feel are necessary. Personally I hate them and I didn't agree to any sort of bucks party before my wedding. On this occasion a group of eight of us, naturally with Hamish one of us, went out drinking. Early in the evening I recall challenging one of our party to a drinking competition with scotch whiskey as the basis for the challenge. We each ordered whiskey and I said, "And I'll have a bottle of soda too, please," and my fellow competitor said, "And you'll nay be needing that tonight." I was not good at drinking whiskey without a bit of dilution and I'm afraid I lost that little competition hands down.

The evening degenerated into a fairly rowdy affair and at 11.30, closing time for the pubs, one of our party suggested that we now had to make a decision as to whether we threw Hamish, the bridegroom of the next day, into the River Dee or the River Don. In Perth you have the choice of those two rivers. At Easter time, both rivers are very, very cold indeed. We went down to the River Dee and Hamish was duly grabbed and dragged into the water. He resisted very strongly and one guy got him by the ankle and said, "If you don't stop struggling, I'm going to twist your ankle." Hamish continued to struggle so this guy twisted his ankle. Eventually he was thrown into the water. Hamish and I eventually got back to our rooms and the next morning when Hamish got out of bed he put his right foot on the floor and let out a scream of pain. His ankle was swollen up and he could barely walk. Three hours later he was due to walk down the aisle. Quite understandably his bride was furious with him and with all of us. Poor Hamish had great difficulty in getting down the aisle but somehow managed it. Those bucks parties really are damn stupid.

Whilst talking about bucks parties, I remember one in Basutoland where some guy was knee-roped by the half-drunken mob and the local meat inspector had brought all his implements of trade along and this poor guy was stamped in green all over every part of his anatomy with the letters "Not fit for consumption". The green dye used by meat inspectors is almost impossible to wash off flesh and so I'm not sure how long it took for him to get all the dye off his body.

Hamish had done an Economics Degree at one of the Scots universities before going down to Cambridge to do the Colonial Service Course. He told me a story of his student days when a group of them had an illicit whiskey still on his grandmother's farm outside Perth. She was all but stone deaf so they set up this still in the attic of one of the farm houses and they used to go down on weekends and have hilarious and uproariously noisy parties in the attic with the whiskey still supplying the booze. His grandmother never knew or found out what was going on. When they had finished university they decided it would be wise to dismantle the still, which they did.

After leaving Hamish and his bride to hobble off on their honeymoon, I went back to Edinburgh and had another week with Morag and Ann. It really was a most enjoyable stay but, as is always the case, good things must come to an end and I went back to Cambridge for my last term. Morag was a prolific letter writer. In those days it was possible for her to post a letter to me in Edinburgh and so long as it was in the post box before 5pm it would be in my pigeonhole at Queens' College by the time I got up the next morning. That was 1954 and it is quite remarkable because that post was not being carried by air but came down on the Edinburgh-London Express which got to London in time for the postal services to connect with all the feeder services out into the counties. Quite remarkable. Morag sometimes wrote me letters in excess of twenty pages. I wish I could find some of them because I don't know what she talked about to fill up twenty pages but neither of us ever got bored. I wrote a lot to her as well but I could never match the length of letter that she seemed to be able to write.

Morag

Third Term, Exams and the Spring Flowers Come Out

In the third term at Cambridge the weather gradually started to warm up and the spring flowers came out. Spring in the UK is beautiful indeed, particularly when all the bulbs send up their blooms. On various occasions friends came to visit. On one occasion Hamish's sister came to Cambridge to visit him. She was a pretty girl in her late teens and very vivacious. Hamish was extremely annoyed with Ian Butler because Ian was in St John's College with Hamish and Hamish caught Ian with a rope dangled out of the window and his sister halfway up on her way to his room. Hamish took it extremely seriously and remained angry with Ian for a long time afterwards. We all thought it was rather funny and it's one of those episodes that you remember. You have to give credit for the resourcefulness of both Ian and Hamish's sister, and the image of Hamish leaning out of his window and seeing this rope dangling from Ian's window with his sister halfway up was an extremely funny one.

We wrote our exams and I was happy with my results and then it was time for the May Ball. Most of the colleges at Cambridge have a May Ball every second year. When I was at Cambridge there were twenty-three colleges so each year there would be about twelve to fourteen colleges holding May Balls. To be able to attend a May Ball at either Oxford or Cambridge is one of the dreams of most girls, and Gail was no exception.

Many years later Beverley, my daughter, was lucky enough to be invited to an Oxford May Ball by a King's College chorister she met on a train (who later stayed with us in Australia) and, several years later, to a Cambridge May Ball by a fellow she met on a bus. So amongst the family, three of the five of us attended May Balls.

The May Ball

Queens' College was not having a May Ball in the year that I was there so I went to the Pembroke College Ball because that's where my good friend Robin Cherry was in residence. Morag came down from Edinburgh for the Ball which was nice and we were a party of four couples. The Ball was held in the main hall and as is the tradition we danced and partied right through the night. It is traditional that with the rising of the sun you get into a punt and if you are capable of doing so, you punt up to Granchester, a distance of about four miles which entails one hell of a lot of hard work at that time of the morning, particularly in view of the fact that you have to punt all the way back again. One couple was very reluctant to punt with us and became quite annoyed with us for insisting that they do so. They eventually caught a taxi up to Granchester. We had our breakfast at Granchester and then we punted back. It was a beautiful day and it was good fun but by the time we got back to our rooms, all of us were pretty well finished. We all went off to sleep it off. Morag had to catch the train back to Edinburgh that night which meant getting down to London in time to catch the overnight express so she, poor thing, had to be on a train by five and then catch her connection up to Edinburgh.

I believe that one of the reasons why an invite to a May Ball is so prized by so many girls is the fact that Oxford and Cambridge are the universities where so many of the elite and future successful students are groomed. A girl, certainly in those days, was brought up to believe that making a good and prosperous match with some young man was a very important element of life. It was still the era of the female being the housewife. The Deb season in the UK is really the way in which the elite young of Britain are given an opportunity to find their partners. The Deb season in England in particular still persists and the so-called "bringing out" of the girl is something that goes back into past centuries. I'm sure it is great fun but there is such a lot of snobbery attached to it.

I Leave Cambridge with some Sadness but Look Forward to my Return to Africa and Lesotho

After the May Ball it was time to pack up and leave Cambridge. I did so with mixed feelings because in many ways I had missed Africa, although I greatly enjoyed my time at Cambridge and appreciated how much it had benefited me. I had been advised that I was definitely being sent back to Basutoland and I knew that when I got there I would be going back to many old friends and would be well received and I was going to have a good time.

Back to see Morag in Edinburgh Before Leaving the UK

After packing up my things and storing them in a friend's flat I set off for Edinburgh to spend time with Morag. I stayed in Ann and Morag's flat and I can recall that Ann departed on some trip leaving Morag and me alone in the flat. We didn't get up to outrageous behaviour but the landlady was advised by some neighbour that Morag was behaving in an immoral way and after I left Morag was given notice. The era was one of very different attitudes to those which exist today, half a century later.

The Tyranny of Distance — Morag and I Never Married

By the end of my stay in Edinburgh Morag and I were pretty sure that we did want to ultimately get married but after I returned to Africa problems developed because Morag was an only child, her mother was a semi-invalid and not healthy and her mother and father raised all sorts of objections. Morag tells me that her father said he didn't think it appropriate that she should go to Africa and live in a mud hut and her mother continually maintained that she was not at all well and that she didn't know that she would be able to live out the time between Morag's visits to her once she went to Africa. I guess it was a pretty difficult situation for Morag. After I had returned to Africa and had been away for a couple of years without seeing her we ultimately decided that it just was not going to be a feasible proposition. I know that Morag is the sort of person who would have had great difficulty had her mother died whilst she was away and in circumstances where her mother had put all this pressure on her. At the time you feel pretty sorry for yourself but you get over these things and I ultimately had a very happy married life and Morag married a doctor and lived in Leeds. I visited Morag in Edinburgh in 1958 when I was on overseas leave. We had three days together. Thereafter I cut ties with her in a rather brutal way but it was for the best; we were in danger of becoming two lonely people living 10,000 miles apart and quite possibly seeing each other at four-year intervals. No fast air services in those days. Our relationship endangered the prospects of both of us doing the natural thing: finding a partner, getting married and having children. I lost contact with her in the sixties.

Reflections 60 years later

Four years from the time of my return to Lesotho, Morag was going out with the doctor just mentioned whom she eventually married, but she was still at the time of my visit not even engaged.

I went to see her in Edinburgh and we spent a couple of days together. It was quite formal. Then she came to the station to see me on my way and we embraced and kissed. And in that last kiss all the old electricity returned for both of us.

It was awful but that kiss remains in my mind to this day and I believe the same would apply to her. I never contacted her again. I think it was best. I was about to go to a country ten thousand miles away with no prospect of us seeing one another for four years.

Yes, these had been wonderful years. And I still miss those after-dinner coffee discussions at Cambridge. There were six of us who casually met a few times a week and just talked.

One of our group was associated with the nuclear capabilities which South Africa developed in collaboration with Israel in the late 1960s. Robin, another of group, was under great pressure to join the team involved in nuclear exploration. He rejected all these offers on moral grounds.

Robin became the physicist working with Christiaan Barnard in Cape Town when the first heart transplant was successfully undertaken by Barnard and he travelled to the USA with Barnard on occasion. Robin was eventually poached by France and put on some project based in Majorca. He spent six months of the year in Majorca and six months with his family in Cape Town. Inevitably the outcome was that he went off with a French colleague and divorced his South African wife.

It was an interesting group because most of us were very opposed to the South African apartheid policy but one or two were uncompromising advocates of the importance of supporting the policy. This difference in political views never seemed to affect our friendships and after a discussion which would probably have involved apartheid, we probably went for a curry at a local Indian restaurant.

Such is the irony of life.

How very lucky I was to have all those experiences with all academic and accommodation expenses paid for by the British Government.

www.ingramcontent.com/pod-product-compliance
Lightning Source LLC
Chambersburg PA
CBHW072015290426
44109CB00018B/2249